leap 1

LISTENING AND SPEAKING

DR. KEN BEATTY

C0-BPA-568

Pearson

Product Owner
Stephan Leduc

Managing Editor
Sharnee Chait

Project Editor
Linda Barton

Proofreader
Sheryl Curtis

Rights and Permissions Coordinator
Aude Maggiori

Text Rights and Permissions
Rachel Irwin

Art Director
Hélène Cousineau

Graphic Design Coordinator
Estelle Cuillerier

Book and Cover Design
Frédérique Bouvier

Book Layout
Marquis Interscript

Cover Photos
Getty Images © Hero Images
Shutterstock © Rawpixel.com

Dedication

To those teachers, in my lectures around the world, who take time to ask questions; ours is a profession that never stops learning.

The publisher wishes to thank the following people for their helpful comments and suggestions:

Kimberly Burrell, Renison University College at University of Waterloo

Jennifer Carioto, Algonquin College

Chris Kelly, Vanwest College

Heather MacLaren, North Island College

Laura Parker, University of Oklahoma

Sheri Rhodes, Mount Royal University

Laurie Thain, St. Giles International

Margaret Wardell, Renison University College at University of Waterloo

© ÉDITIONS DU RENOUVEAU PÉDAGOGIQUE INC. (ERPI), 2017
ERPI publishes and distributes PEARSON ELT products in Canada.

1611 Crémazie Boulevard East, 10th Floor
Montréal, Québec H2M 2P2
Canada
Telephone: 1 800 263-3678
Fax: 1 514 334-4720
information@pearsonerpi.com
pearsonerpi.com

DANGER
PHOTOCOPYING KILLS BOOKS

All rights reserved.
No part of this publication may be reproduced, stored in a retrieval system, or transmitted in any form or by any means, electronic, mechanical, photocopying, recording, or otherwise without the prior written permission of ÉDITIONS DU RENOUVEAU PÉDAGOGIQUE INC.

Registration of copyright—Bibliothèque et Archives nationales du Québec, 2017
Registration of copyright—Library and Archives Canada, 2017

Printed in Canada   123456789 HLN 20 19 18 17
ISBN 978-2-7613-8346-2   138346 ABCD   OF10

Access
My eLab
leap 1

TO REGISTER

❶ Go to **http://mybookshelf.pearsonerpi.com**

❷ Follow the instructions. When asked for your access code, please type the code provided underneath the blue sticker.

❸ To access **My eLab** at any time, go to http://mybookshelf.pearsonerpi.com. **Bookmark this page for quicker access.**

Access to My eLab is valid for 12 months from the date of registration.

WARNING! This book CANNOT BE RETURNED if the access code has been uncovered.

Note: Once you have registered, you will need to join your online class. Ask your teacher to provide you with the class ID.

TEACHER Access Code

To obtain an access code for My eLab, please contact your Pearson ELT consultant.

1 800 263-3678, ext. 2
pearsonerpi.com/help

W138346 (A38399)

4812

INTRODUCTION

Welcome to *LEAP 1: Listening and Speaking*. Much of what you understand about the world comes from what you hear and you refine that understanding by engaging in questions and discussions. *LEAP 1* provides language skills necessary for success in college and university where you need to quickly capture the details of lectures and discussions, take notes, and ask questions. A cross-curricular approach gives you opportunities to explore new ideas from different academic disciplines including architecture, history, and statistics. Within these disciplines are topics as diverse as extinctions, genetics, inventions and the sharing economy. Along the way, the Pearson Global Scale of English (GSE) structures *LEAP 1's* learning goals as you build your high-frequency vocabulary with essential words from the Longman Communication 3000 and the Academic Word List.

LEAP 1: Listening and Speaking helps you deal with challenging ideas. Different listening genres include interviews, lectures, and podcasts, as well as graphic organizers in each chapter. These all help you work toward the listening and speaking demands you encounter. Through carefully structured activities, you build your vocabulary and listening comprehension. Each chapter features focuses on listening, speaking, critical thinking, grammar, and academic survival skills which support warm-up and final assignments. My eLab exercises and documents give you opportunities to reinforce and build on what you learn.

I am certain that *LEAP 1: Listening and Speaking* will be a key stepping-stone on your path to academic success.

ACKNOWLEDGEMENTS

The entire *LEAP* series is a grand collaboration fuelled by teachers who share time and ideas about student needs to help develop these print and online materials; my deepest thanks to all those teachers with whom I spoke at colleges, universities, and conferences. Thanks also to my gracious and supportive editors, Sharnee Chait and Linda Barton; their countless suggestions shaped this book. I'm grateful to the entire Pearson Canada team and Pearson teams in other countries I've had the privilege to visit including, this past year, Bulgaria, Colombia, Ecuador, Mexico, Peru, Poland, and the USA. And, as always, my thanks to Julia Williams, who pioneered the *LEAP* series.

Dr. Ken Beatty, Bowen Island, Canada

HIGHLIGHTS

Gearing Up uses images to spark critical thinking, reflection, and discussion about the chapter topic.

The **overview** outlines the chapter objectives.

Vocabulary Build strengthens comprehension of key vocabulary words and reinforces them through tasks. Appendix 2 allows you to see how these words are rated in the Longman Communication 3000 and the Academic Word List.

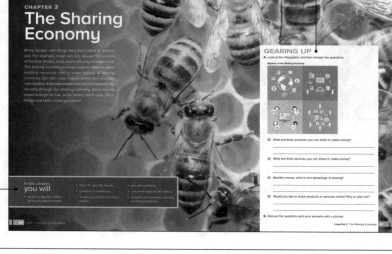

Focus on Critical Thinking introduces you to strategies for thinking critically about what you hear and how to apply these strategies to listening and speaking tasks.

Before You Listen activities elicit your prior knowledge of a subject and stimulate interest.

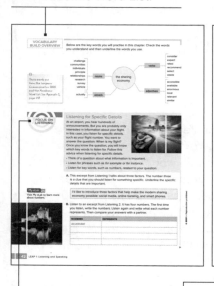

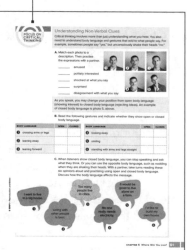

After You Listen activities give you an opportunity to reflect on personal or larger issues related to what you have heard.

Focus on Listening develops specific skills you need to fully understand the content and structure of lectures and discussions.

Each chapter has a **Pronunciation** sidebar that provides hints and tips. You can complete pronunciation exercises on My eLab.

While You Listen activities engage you in a variety of active listening strategies, including taking notes.

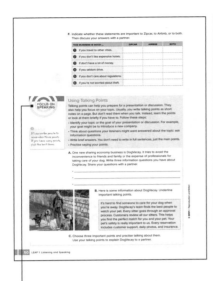

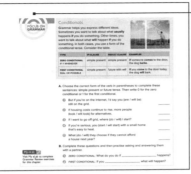

Focus on Grammar reviews important grammar features that you can apply in the warm-up and final assignments.

The **listenings**, including one video per chapter, come from various sources: debates, interviews, lectures, and podcasts.

Academic Survival Skill helps you develop essential skills for academic coursework.

Focus on Speaking develops the skills you need to effectively discuss issues, ask questions, and express opinions.

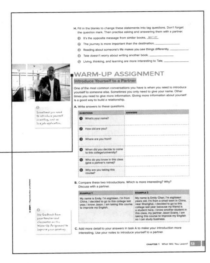

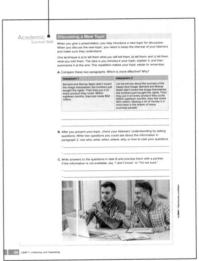

The **Warm-Up Assignment** prepares you for the Final Assignment.

References to **My eLab** provide practice and additional content.

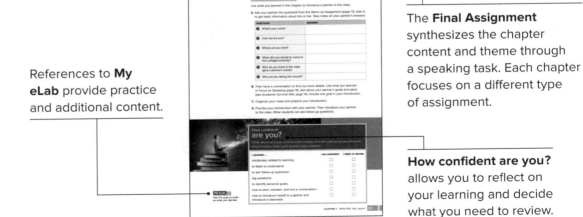

The **Final Assignment** synthesizes the chapter content and theme through a speaking task. Each chapter focuses on a different type of assignment.

How confident are you? allows you to reflect on your learning and decide what you need to review.

SCOPE AND SEQUENCE

CHAPTER	LISTENING	CRITICAL THINKING	SPEAKING

CHAPTER 1
WHAT WILL YOU LEARN?
 	
SUBJECT AREAS: education, technology
	• Listening to understand
	  - Learn tips to help your understanding
		• Asking follow-up questions
		  - Use reduced-form questions
			• Starting, maintaining, and ending a conversation
			• Pronunciation: Intonation in *wh-* questions

CHAPTER 2
THE JOY OF INVENTING
 	
SUBJECT AREAS: engineering, innovation
	• Listening for main points
	  - Identify key words and ideas
		• Sketching what you hear
		  - Understand things in new ways
			• Using linking words
			• Pronunciation: Stress in nouns and verbs

CHAPTER 3
THE SHARING ECONOMY
 	
SUBJECT AREAS: business, economics
	• Listening for specific details
	  - Find information by listening for key words and phrases
		• Questioning assumptions
		  - Try to see potential problems
			• Using talking points
			• Pronunciation: Dates, times and numbers

CHAPTER 4
YOUR DREAM JOB
 	
SUBJECT AREAS: economics, statistics
	• Listening to compare
	  - Listen for adjectives, comparatives, and superlatives
		• Recognizing point of view
		  - Listen for clues in the title and main points
			• Disagreeing politely
			• Pronunciation: Emphasis on key words in a sentence

CHAPTER 5
WHERE WILL YOU LIVE?
 	
SUBJECT AREAS: architecture, sociology
	• Listening for opinions
	  - Identify key words to decide whether an opinion is supported by facts
		• Understanding non-verbal clues
		  - Use body language to enhance understanding
			• Expressing an opinion
			• Pronunciation: Words ending in the letter *-s*

CHAPTER 6
EARTH, YOUR HOME
 	
SUBJECT AREAS: biology, history
	• Listening to infer the meaning of words
	  - Use the context to infer meaning of words
		• Connecting new ideas to what you know
		  - Make connections to familiar and unfamiliar ideas
			• Giving instructions
			• Pronunciation: Two ways to pronounce *th-*

CHAPTER 7
BE A PERFECT HUMAN
 	
SUBJECT AREAS: genetics, medicine
	• Listening for details about charts
	  - Learn tips to help understand a chart
		• Predicting to listen effectively
		  - Identify the topic and think of questions as you listen
			• Structuring a presentation
			• Pronunciation: Words with silent letters

CHAPTER 8
THE SIXTH EXTINCTION
 	
SUBJECT AREAS: geography, paleontology
	• Listening for sequence
	  - Identify key words and phrases
		• Paraphrasing to understand
		  - Learn strategies for paraphrasing in a conversation
			• Making and responding to suggestions
			• Pronunciation: The *-ed* ending

GRAMMAR	ACADEMIC SURVIVAL SKILL	ASSIGNMENTS	My eLab
• Tag questions	• Identifying personal goals - Plan how to get things done	• Introducing yourself to a partner • Introducing a classmate	
• Adverbs of frequency	• Discussing a new topic - Introduce your topic, explain it, and summarize it	• Explaining an invention to a partner • Discussing an invention with a partner	

• Count and non-count nouns	• Using mind maps to take notes
	  - Record what you hear and read
		• Examining a sharing economy business
		• Presenting a sharing economy business
			• Online practice for each chapter:
			  - More comprehension exercises for the listenings
			  - Vocabulary review
			  - Grammar practice
			  - Speaking focus review
			  - Pronunciation practice
			  - Chapter test

• Prepositions of time and place	• Working with a partner
	  - Learn tips to work effectively
		• Describing your dream job
		• Comparing two jobs
			• Additional online listenings:
			  - Extra listening with comprehension and critical thinking questions

• Conditionals (zero and first)	• Working in a group
	  - Learn tips for working in groups
		• Presenting your opinion
		• Discussing your opinion
			• Study resources in Documents including:
			  - All audio and video clips from the coursebook
			  - Irregular Verbs List

• Asking questions using modals	• Asking questions in a lecture - Learn tips on when and how to ask questions	• Preparing a set of instructions • Presenting and discussing instructions in a group	
• Present perfect tense	• Talking with graphic organizers - Learn strategies to use graphic organizers effectively	• Talking about a new habit • Discussing new habits in a group	
• Simple past and present perfect tenses	• Taking part in a panel discussion - Learn how to conduct a panel discussion	• Discussing an extinction event • Sharing ideas in a panel discussion	

TABLE OF CONTENTS

CHAPTER 1
What Will You Learn?

In school and on your own, you spend your life learning. In many cases, when you are young, you have little choice about what you learn in school. But, as you get older, you make decisions about what to study based on what you are good at and what interests you. You also spend more time learning outside of school. These choices influence what you will do for a career. How do you decide what to learn?

In this chapter, you will

- learn vocabulary related to learning;
- listen to understand;
- ask follow-up questions;
- review tag questions;
- identify personal goals;
- learn how to start, maintain, and end a conversation;
- introduce yourself to a partner and introduce a classmate.

GEARING UP

A. Consider things you would like to do. Look at the diagram and then answer the questions.

① Winning a sports competition is a specific goal. What is a smaller, achievable step to help you get there?

_____

_____

② Success in education is often measured by passing courses. What is another measure of success when you study?

_____

_____

③ What is something difficult for most people that you think is realistic for you?

_____

_____

④ *Timely* means you know you can complete something in a certain time frame. What's something you would like to get done in the next year?

_____

_____

B. Discuss the questions and your answers with a partner.

VOCABULARY BUILD OVERVIEW

Below are the key words you will practise in this chapter. Check the words you understand and then underline the words you use.

These words are from the Longman Communication 3000 and the Academic Word List. See Appendix 2, page 158.

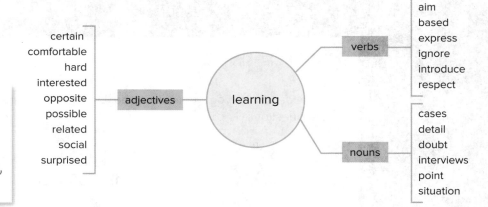

adjectives
certain
comfortable
hard
interested
opposite
possible
related
social
surprised

learning

verbs
aim
based
express
ignore
introduce
respect

nouns
cases
detail
doubt
interviews
point
situation

FOCUS ON LISTENING

Listening to Understand

There are many different reasons for why you listen. For example, you may listen in a dentist's waiting room for your name to be called. In this example, you are not trying to understand your name. But in most situations, the most important reason to listen is to understand what is being said. Here are some tips to help you when you listen to understand.

• Pay attention. Silence your phone, close your laptop, and look directly at the speaker.

• Use body language to show when you understand and when you don't understand. Nod, smile, and use words like "yes," "I see," and "OK," when you understand. When you don't understand, frown in concentration and tilt your head. The speaker may take these signs and try harder to explain the topic.

• Ask follow-up questions about things you do not understand: "Could you explain that, please?"

• Ask follow-up questions by paraphrasing (saying in other words) ideas you are not sure about. This means you repeat the idea in a new way to check what the speaker means: "By *destination*, do you mean a place?"

A. Listen to six statements. Each statement is spoken three times. Write a follow-up question for each one. Then practise saying the statements and asking the questions with a partner.

1 _____

2 _____

3 _____

4 _____

5 _____

6 _____

© ERPI • Reproduction prohibited

B. Listen to six more statements. These statements are also repeated three times. Paraphrase each statement and then compare them with a partner.

1 _____
_____

2 _____
_____

3 _____
_____

4 _____
_____

5 _____
_____

6 _____
_____

FOCUS ON CRITICAL THINKING

❗ In a lecture, a speaker will often say, "If you have questions, please interrupt." Or "If you have questions, please save them until the end."

Asking Follow-up Questions

When you listen, think of questions you want answered. Sometimes your questions are answered as the speaker continues to speak. Sometimes you can wait until the speaker is finished to ask questions. But other times, you could interrupt—or break into the conversation—to get the information you need. Asking follow-up questions in a reduced form is the best way to interrupt because the questions can be a single word: *who, what, when, where, why,* and *how.*

Example: **JAY:** I went for a long walk on the weekend.
TOM: Where did you go for a long walk on the weekend?

Tom's question is too long. It would be better to use the reduced form: *Where?* There is no need to repeat the details and this is a shorter interruption.

Read these examples and rewrite the questions in a reduced form.

QUESTIONS IN REDUCED FORM

1 Soon it will be time for dinner.
When will we have dinner? _____ *When?* _____

❗ Sometimes you use other words like "really" to ask questions in a reduced form. They may show surprise, or that you are listening, but no answer is expected.

2 There is something that I need to tell you.
Can you tell me what it is you need to say? _____

3 I need to find a store that sells chilli peppers.
How will you find a store that sells chilli peppers? _____

4 I can't meet you tomorrow afternoon.
Can you tell me why you can't meet me tomorrow afternoon? _____

5 We are going to meet at six o'clock.
OK, six o'clock, but where will we meet? _____

© ERPI • Reproduction prohibited

LISTENING ❶ An Interview about Goals

An interview is a good way to collect information. In Listening 1, Jack interviews Anna to find out about her goals. When you answer interview questions, ask about words and questions you don't understand. Pay attention to how Anna makes sure she understands each interview question.

VOCABULARY BUILD

In the following exercises, explore key words from Listening 1.

A. Match each word to its definition.

WORDS		DEFINITIONS
❶ cases (n.)	___b___	a) difficult
❷ hard (adj.)	_____	b) situations
❸ introduce (v.)	_____	c) connected in some way
❹ possible (adj.)	_____	d) admire someone or something
❺ related (adj.)	_____	e) present one person to another
❻ respect (v.)	_____	f) able to be done

B. Fill in the blanks with the correct words to complete the sentences.

hard	interview	possible	respect

❶ She wanted to go to Italy but didn't know if it was _____*possible*_____.

❷ It was a _____ question and she didn't know the answer.

❸ The _____ was to get a part-time job at the coffee shop.

❹ You need to _____ the books and not leave them on the floor.

C. What do the words in bold mean to you? Complete the sentences.

❶ What is a career that is **related** to your studies?

   A related career is _____

❷ What **possible** trip might you take someday?

   A possible trip I might take is _____

❸ Which job do you think is **hard** work?

   I think _____

❹ Who did you **introduce** recently?

   I introduced _____

© ERPI • Reproduction prohibited

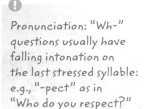

Pronunciation: "Wh-"
questions usually have
falling intonation on
the last stressed syllable:
e.g., "-pect" as in
"Who do you respect?"

My eLab ✎

Visit My eLab to complete
a pronunciation exercise.

Before You Listen

A. Listening 1 includes these interview questions. Write your own answers as short notes. Then take turns practising the questions and answers with a partner.

1 What is your educational goal? _____

2 Do you have a short-term goal? _____

3 Where do you want to go? _____

4 Why do you want to go there? _____

_____

5 Who do you respect? _____

6 When will you achieve your goals? _____

7 What can help you reach your goals? _____

_____

B. What is something that interferes (gets in the way) with reaching your goals? Discuss with your partner. Then paraphrase your partner's answer.

_____

_____

While You Listen

C. The first time you listen, try to understand the general idea and fill in the answers that Anna gives in the interview with Jack. Listen again and write reduced form follow-up questions to each of her answers. Listen a third time to check your answers.

INTERVIEW QUESTIONS	ANNA'S ANSWERS	FOLLOW-UP QUESTIONS
1 What is your educational goal?	*to become a lawyer*	*Why?*
2 Do you have a short-term goal?		
3 Where do you want to go?		
4 Why do you want to go there?		
5 Who do you respect?	*Jane Austen*	
6 When will you achieve your goals?		
7 What can help you reach your goals?		

After You Listen

D. Choose the phrase that best completes each sentence, according to the listening.

1. Jack is probably doing a survey _____.
   a) for his own interest
   b) as a class project
   c) to become a lawyer

2. Jack's university goals are _____.
   a) the same as Anna's
   b) different from Anna's
   c) close to Anna's

3. Short-term goals refer to goals that _____.
   a) take one school term
   b) might take years
   c) can be done soon

4. Jack makes a mistake and thinks Anna wants to learn _____.
   a) to drive
   b) to dive
   c) to speak Italian

5. The question on respect is about someone _____.
   a) you are afraid of
   b) who writes books
   c) you want to be like

6. Anna can reach her goals with _____.
   a) time, money, and lessons
   b) trips, education, and support
   c) lessons, training, and money

E. Look at the reduced form follow-up questions you wrote in While You Listen, task C. Turn them into full questions you would ask to help you understand. Then ask a partner the questions. Switch and guess the answers.

INTERVIEW QUESTIONS	FULL QUESTIONS
1 What is your educational goal?	*Why do you want to become a lawyer?*
2 Do you have a short-term goal?	
3 Where do you want to go?	
4 Why do you want to go there?	
5 Who do you respect?	
6 When will you achieve your goals?	
7 What can help you reach your goals?	

© **ERPI** • Reproduction prohibited

© **ERPI** • Reproduction prohibited

FOCUS ON GRAMMAR

Tag Questions

You can use tag questions to turn statements into questions. You often use tag questions to check information that you think is true.

Form tag questions with an auxiliary verb such as *be* or *have*. Use contractions for negative tag questions.

Examples: There is a test today, **isn't** there?
You have a test, **haven't** you?

If the statement does not include an auxiliary, use *do*.

Example: You like English, **don't** you?

If the statement is positive, use a negative question tag. If the statement is negative, use a positive question tag.

Examples: **It is** time for lunch (positive), **isn't it** (negative)?
It isn't time for lunch (negative), **is it** (positive)?

The question tag after "I am" is "aren't I":
I'm next, aren't I?

A. Change these sentences into tag questions. Use either a positive or a negative tag. Then write an answer for each question. Add two of your own tag questions and answers.

1 He is interested in birds, *isn't he?*

No, he isn't./Yes, he is.

2 They are friends, _____

_____

3 Jack wants to achieve his goals, _____

_____

4 Anna isn't a writer, _____

_____

5 Jack likes to learn, _____

_____

6 They don't scuba dive, _____

_____

7 _____

_____

_____

8 _____

_____

 My eLab

Visit My eLab to complete Grammar Review exercises for this chapter.

B. Practise asking and answering the tag questions with a partner.

LISTENING ❷   Enjoy the Journey

Birdwatchers come in two types. The first type rushes around trying to record as many sightings of new birds as possible. The second type goes out into nature, takes a picnic, relaxes, and looks for birds but is not disappointed if none appear. The difference is a focus on *completing* a task or *enjoying yourself* while you do the task. What kind of person are you?

VOCABULARY BUILD

In the following exercises, explore key words from Listening 2.

A. Choose the word or phrase that best completes each sentence. Key words are in bold.

1 **Aim** to find a job you _____ every day of your life.

   a) change   b) hate   c) enjoy

2 I used to make long lists and _____ my life in **detail**.

   a) plan   b) waste   c) choose

3 It's wrong to focus on _____ and **ignore** all the colors, smells, and tastes of India.

   a) everything   b) anything   c) one thing

4 My book says something _____ and has the **opposite** message.

   a) often   b) different   c) similar

5 It's an important **point** that you _____ forget.

   a) should   b) can't   c) must

B. The words *interested* and *surprised* are both adjectives with root words that are nouns and verbs. Match each word to its definition.

WORDS		DEFINITIONS
1 interest (n.)	_____	a) unexpected event
2 interest (v.)	_____	b) startle someone with something unexpected
3 interested (adj.)	_____	c) feeling of wanting to know more about something
4 surprise (n.)	_____	d) get someone excited about something
5 surprise (v.)	_____	e) feeling of shock about something
6 surprised (adj.)	_____	f) being curious about something

C. What do the words in bold mean to you? Complete the sentences.

1 What is something new you're **interested** in?

Something new I'm interested in is _____

_____

© **ERPI** • Reproduction prohibited

② What's a small problem you usually **ignore**?

I usually ignore _____

_____

③ What's something that **surprised** you this week?

Something that surprised me _____

_____

_____

④ What's a **point** you discussed with friends?

A point I discussed _____

_____

_____

⑤ What's a **detail** you often forget?

I often forget _____

_____

Before You Listen

A. Read this excerpt from Listening 2. In it Sam Tate says "the journey is often more important than the destination." Do you know what he means? Discuss with a partner.

> I explain that the *journey* is often more important than the *destination*. For example, a few days ago I was talking to someone who told me her big dream was to see the Taj Mahal, in India, and to take a selfie there.

B. Write two follow-up questions about the second statement.

FOLLOW-UP QUESTION 1: _____

_____

FOLLOW-UP QUESTION 2: _____

_____

C. Listening 2 mentions John James Audubon (1785–1851). He is famous for his discovery of new birds and for his paintings of them. Read this list of goals and choose those you think Audubon might have wanted to accomplish.

- ☐ become a sea captain
- ☐ spend time in nature
- ☐ become famous around the world
- ☐ learn how to draw and paint

© **ERPI** • Reproduction prohibited

While You Listen

D. The first time you listen, try to understand the general idea. Listen a second time to complete the sentences in your own words. Listen a third time to check your answers.

Sam Tate's ideas	Your words
1 Sam Tate's book is different ...	*It's the opposite message from similar books. The journey is more important than the destination.*
2 A woman wanted to take a selfie at the Taj Mahal ...	She will miss
3 Tate didn't always feel this way.	He used to make long He used to plan
4 Reading about John James Audubon ...	Reading about Audubon changed
5 Audubon painted and ...	Audubon did paintings of He discovered _____ new ones.
6 Audubon was interested ...	He was interested in
7 Audubon's father's goals for him ...	But Audubon got sick on
8 Tate's future plans ...	He might write _____ and _____ are more interesting to Tate.

After You Listen

E. Check your follow-up questions in Before You Listen, task B. Were your questions answered in Listening 2? Write the answers here.

1 _____

_____

2 _____

_____

F. Review your answers in Before You Listen, task C. Were your choices correct?

G. Indicate whether these statements are true or false, according to the listening.

Statements	True	False
1 Sam Tate wrote a book called *No More Goals*.		
2 The book is about all the places you should see and foods you should eat.		
3 Focusing on the Taj Mahal might mean you ignore all the colors, smells, and tastes of India.		
4 Tate used to plan his life in detail.		
5 Tate suggests you should follow other people's plans.		
6 Tate is more interested in living, thinking, and learning than in writing another book.		

© ERPI • Reproduction prohibited

H. Fill in the blanks to change these statements into tag questions. Don't forget the question mark. Then practise asking and answering them with a partner.

1 It's the opposite message from similar books, _isn't it?_

2 The journey is more important than the destination, _____

3 Reading about someone's life makes you see things differently, _____

4 Tate doesn't worry about writing another book, _____

5 Living, thinking, and learning are more interesting to Tate, _____

WARM-UP ASSIGNMENT
Introduce Yourself to a Partner

One of the most common conversations you have is when you need to introduce yourself to someone else. Sometimes you only need to give your name. Other times you need to give more information. Giving more information about yourself is a good way to build a relationship.

> Sometimes you need to introduce yourself in writing, such as in a job application.

A. Write answers to these questions.

QUESTIONS	ANSWERS
1 What's your name?	
2 How old are you?	
3 Where are you from?	
4 When did you decide to come to this college/university?	
5 Who do you know in this class (give a partner's name)?	
6 Why are you taking this course?	

B. Compare these two introductions. Which is more interesting? Why? Discuss with a partner.

EXAMPLE 1	EXAMPLE 2
My name is Emily. I'm eighteen. I'm from China. I decided to go to this college last year. I know Jason. I am taking this course to improve my English.	My name is Emily Chan. I'm eighteen years old. I'm from a small town in China, near Shanghai. I decided to go to this college last year because my friend is a student here. I know another student in this class, my partner Jason Evans. I am taking this course to improve my English so I can study business.

> Use feedback from your teacher and classmates on this Warm-Up Assignment to improve your speaking.

C. Add more detail to your answers in task A to make your introduction more interesting. Use your notes to introduce yourself to a partner.

© **ERPI** • Reproduction prohibited

Academic
Survival Skill

Identifying Personal Goals

Listening 2 suggested goals can sometimes distract you from enjoying other things, but sometimes you need to plan to get things done. Research shows that people who write a list of things they want to do, get more done than people who do not. But you need to keep your list from five to seven items.

A. Think about your goals in life. Read the questions and write your answers in point form. After, discuss with a partner.

GOALS IN LIFE	QUESTIONS	YOUR ANSWERS
CAREER	What do you want to do as a career?	
CULTURE	Would you like to learn more about the arts, such as painting and music? Would you like to learn skills in these or other artistic areas?	
EDUCATION	What skills do you want to learn for your own interest or to improve your career opportunities?	
FITNESS	Would you like to be in better shape? Would you like to learn a new sport?	
FUN	What would you like to do for enjoyment? Is there a new experience or skill you would like to have?	
OUTLOOK	Do you have attitudes that you would like to change or improve?	
VOLUNTEER	What would you like to do to help others? You may learn a new skill while you do.	

© **ERPI** • Reproduction prohibited

B. A goal without a plan is just a wish. Choose a goal from task A, and using the SMART criteria from Gearing Up (page 3), write a plan. Then discuss your plan with a partner.

SMART GOAL CRITERIA	YOUR PLAN
SPECIFIC: Can you shorten your goal to make it clearer?	
MEASURABLE: How will you know when you have met your goal?	
ACHIEVABLE: What skills and hard work do you need to reach your goal?	
REALISTIC: How do you know you can reach your goal?	
TIMELY: When can you achieve your goal? Give a time or date.	

 **LISTENING ③** **How to Learn Anything**

What's the most difficult thing you ever tried to learn? The Massachusetts Institute of Technology (MIT) offers a four-year degree in computer science. Scott Young started what he called "the MIT challenge" to learn everything taught in the degree in twelve months. He used MIT's own online courses. What is a learning challenge you would like to try?

VOCABULARY BUILD

In the following exercises, explore key words from Listening 3.

A. Fill in the blanks with the correct words to complete the paragraph.

comfortable	doubt	situation	social

You might sometimes _____ your ability to learn new things. Most people stick to things they feel _____ doing. But sometimes you find yourself in a _____ where everything is new: for example, a _____ gathering doing something different with new people. When you do learn something new, you feel good about yourself.

© **ERPI** • Reproduction prohibited

B. Read these sentences. Then write the part of speech (adjective, noun, or verb) and the definition of the words in bold. Look up words you don't know in a dictionary.

SENTENCES	PARTS OF SPEECH	DEFINITIONS
❶ There was no **doubt** in my mind that I could do it.	*noun*	*feeling of not knowing something*
❷ And there are **certain** parts of your intelligence that are probably fixed.		
❸ A lot of it is **based** on your past experience.		
❹ I have the ability to **express** just a handful of concepts.		

C. What do the words in bold mean to you? Complete the sentences.

❶ What is something you find easy to **express**?

Something I find easy _____

❷ What's something you're never **certain** about?

I'm never certain _____

❸ What are your interests in music **based** on?

My interests are based on _____

❹ What's something you **doubt**?

Something I doubt _____

❺ What's your favourite **social** activity?

My favourite _____

My eLab

Visit My eLab to complete Vocabulary Review exercises for this chapter.

Before You Listen

A. Scott Young says he spent a year in four countries, learning Spanish in Spain, Portuguese in Brazil, Mandarin Chinese in China, and Korean in Korea. Write follow-up questions about what Young did.

❶ Who *did he go with (or did he go alone)?* _____

❷ What _____

_____

❸ When _____

_____

❹ Where _____

_____

© **ERPI** • Reproduction prohibited

⑤ Why _____

_____

⑥ How _____

_____

B. When people speak, they often make grammar mistakes and say things in ways that can be difficult to understand. Read this excerpt from Listening 3. Then choose the best paraphrase.

> And if you suddenly go into a situation where you're at the beginning, where you don't speak a language very well, and I no longer understand anything that you're saying, and I have the ability to express just a handful of concepts—and this is a real social situation, this isn't a classroom where the person, you know, is forgiving and understanding—they're kind of like, "Wait, what do you want?" and you're trying to explain it. That's the part that scares most people.

☐ In a real social situation, it's hard to speak another language. It scares people that others are not forgiving and understanding.

☐ In a social situation, I have a handful of concepts and it isn't like a classroom where people ask me what I want.

C. Write a follow-up question to the paraphrase in task B.

_____

_____

While You Listen

D. The first time you listen, try to understand the general idea. Listen a second time to complete the paraphrase of each idea. Listen a third time to check your notes and add details to your paraphrases.

SCOTT YOUNG'S IDEAS	PARAPHRASES
❶ Intelligence is such a huge one that people believe, usually from poor school experiences, that ...	*People believe they're not smart or smart at some things.*
❷ Or, "I'm not good at languages" ... we don't have a positive experience with it ...	People are discouraged because they
❸ People say "you can't change your intelligence."	Some parts of intelligence are fixed but
❹ I was more of a math sort of science person ... a little bit less languages, and used to think, I probably can't learn other languages very easily.	Learning French became
❺ I took a year off, and went to four countries in one year to learn four languages.	His goal was to not speak English

© **ERPI** • Reproduction prohibited

SCOTT YOUNG'S IDEAS	PARAPHRASES
6 So it was Spanish in Spain, Portuguese in Brazil, Mandarin Chinese in China, and Korean in Korea.	*It went well:* • *a decent conversational level in all of them;* • *Korean rustier for conversation;* • *Very comfortable in Spanish.*
7 So I felt that learning a language was not so much of an intellectual challenge as it was a social challenge.	*In a real social situation, it scares people that others are not understanding or forgiving.*
8 That's the part that's hardest for most people to be like, "No, I'm going to keep trying with this, ..."	Learning a language eventually
9 We did have to break character in China a little bit, and in Korea.	Chinese and Korean are
10 Like, it's not a situation where, "OK, now it's over and we're speaking English."	After a short break, it's important to
11 Having a big blog where you've told people that you're going to do this, and you're filming a documentary really helps [keep on task].	Young was motivated by

After You Listen

E. Look at the questions you wrote in Before You Listen, task A. Write answers to the ones that Young answered in the interview.

1 (Who) _____

_____

2 (What) _____

_____

3 (When) _____

_____

4 (Where) _____

_____

5 (Why) _____

_____

6 (How) _____

_____

F. Choose the phrase that best completes each sentence, according to the listening.

1 When Young talks about people's ideas that they cannot learn, he blames _____.

a) schools and other people

b) people who don't try hard enough

© **ERPI** • Reproduction prohibited

2 Young probably chose the four languages because they were _____.

   a) quite different from each other

   b) all easy for beginner learners

3 Young's opinion of intelligence is that it is _____.

   a) fixed and unlikely to change

   b) mostly fixed but possible to change

4 The experience that probably made Young think he could succeed was learning _____.

   a) English in England

   b) French in France

5 A big motivation for Young was that he was also doing a _____.

   a) blog and a documentary

   b) part-time job and a textbook

6 After the MIT challenge and learning four new languages, Young will likely _____.

   a) look for a new challenge

   b) return to study at MIT

G. Write two follow-up questions about Young's year learning four languages? Then practise asking and answering the questions with a partner.

1 _____

   _____

2 _____

   _____

FOCUS ON SPEAKING

Starting, Maintaining and Ending a Conversation

Conversations have three main stages. First, you need to start a conversation with a greeting. Then, as you talk, you need to maintain the conversation by giving feedback to the other speaker. Finally, you need to know how to end a conversation.

START A CONVERSATION

EXAMPLE	TIPS

In Listening 1, Jack begins with, "Excuse me, do you have a minute?"	• Give a general greeting: Hello.
	• Introduce yourself: My name is _____.
	• Ask a question or make a comment.
	  Examples: Could you give me a [request]?
	         I like your [personal remark].
	         I want to talk to you about [introduce a topic].

© ERPI • Reproduction prohibited

▶

MAINTAIN A CONVERSATION

EXAMPLE	TIPS
In Listening 3, Ramit Sethi uses a follow-up question, "OK. And how did it go?"	• Ask follow-up questions: Does that mean _____? • Ask questions to understand: I don't know what you mean by _____? • Change the subject: On another topic, _____.

END A CONVERSATION

EXAMPLE	TIPS

In Listening 2, Tara Jones ends the conversation with, "Well, thanks. It's been great hearing from you."	• Signal that the conversation is over.
	
	  Examples: I really enjoyed talking to you.
	           It was nice to see you again.
	           I will let you go now.

> ❗ The SOFTEN technique helps you create a good impression: **S**mile, **O**pen your posture, **F**orward lean, **T**ouch, **E**ye contact, **N**od.

A. Indicate when you would use each sentence in a conversation.

SENTENCES	START	MAINTAIN	END
❶ That reminds me of something I read today.			
❷ I'm sorry, I have to go now. Bye.			.
❸ Hello, I'm Amir.			
❹ It was great talking with you. Goodbye.			
❺ That's a good point, but I disagree.			
❻ How are you doing?			
❼ Oh, I had better hurry. I'm late for class.			
❽ Hi. Do you have a few moments?			
❾ What did you think of the movie we just saw?			

a tortoise in Galapagos

B. Work with a partner. First, read this conversation.

ELLEN: Hi. I'm Ellen.
MIKE: Hi, Ellen. I'm Mike.
ELLEN: I'd like to go to Galapagos Ecuador and dive with the fish. Any suggestions?
MIKE: You should try to see the tortoises.
ELLEN: That's a good idea. Thanks. I have to go now. Goodbye.

C. Now, follow these points and add ideas to start, maintain, and end a conversation of your own. Practise the conversation together.

• Use your names and introduce yourselves.

• Introduce a goal you have, such as a place you would like to travel.

• Suggest information you might need before the trip.

• End the conversation in a polite way.

© **ERPI** • Reproduction prohibited

FINAL ASSIGNMENT
Introduce a Classmate

Use what you learned in this chapter to introduce a partner to the class.

A. Ask your partner the questions from the Warm-Up Assignment (page 13), task A, to get basic information about him or her. Take notes on your partner's answers.

QUESTIONS	ANSWERS
❶ What's your name?	
❷ How old are you?	
❸ Where are you from?	
❹ When did you decide to come to this college/university?	
❺ Who do you know in this class (give a partner's name)?	
❻ Why are you taking this course?	

B. Then have a conversation to find out more details. Use what you learned in Focus on Speaking (page 19). Ask about your partner's goals and plans (see Academic Survival Skill, page 14). Include one goal in your introduction.

C. Organize your notes and prepare your introduction.

D. Practise your introduction with your partner. Then introduce your partner to the class. Other students can ask follow-up questions.

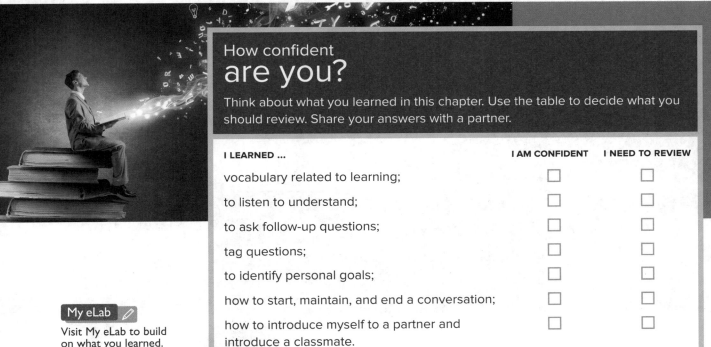

How confident are you?

Think about what you learned in this chapter. Use the table to decide what you should review. Share your answers with a partner.

I LEARNED ...	I AM CONFIDENT	I NEED TO REVIEW
vocabulary related to learning;	☐	☐
to listen to understand;	☐	☐
to ask follow-up questions;	☐	☐
tag questions;	☐	☐
to identify personal goals;	☐	☐
how to start, maintain, and end a conversation;	☐	☐
how to introduce myself to a partner and introduce a classmate.	☐	☐

My eLab ✎
Visit My eLab to build on what you learned.

CHAPTER 2

The Joy of Inventing

From the 14th to the 16th centuries, the Aztecs were great builders and astronomers, but they never developed wheels for transportation. Although they used wheels on children's toys, perhaps wheeled vehicles did not seem useful. The Aztec capital city was on islands on a lake and it was easier to travel by boat. The surrounding mountain paths were also not suited for wheeled transportation. But not using wheels for transportation meant the Aztec did not develop gears and other machine parts. What is necessary for an invention to be successful?

In this chapter, you will

- learn vocabulary related to inventions;

- listen for main points;
- sketch what you hear;
- review adverbs of frequency;
- learn to use linking words;

- learn how to discuss a new topic;
- explain an invention to a partner and then discuss it.

GEARING UP

A. A geodesic dome, often made of glass triangles, is an example of a great invention with limited popularity. Look at the photo and then answer the questions.

Domes of a Botanic Garden in Milwaukee, Wisconsin

1 Have you or someone you know ever seen or visited a geodesic dome? When and where?

_____

_____

2 Why do you think geodesic domes were not invented hundreds of years ago?

_____

_____

3 Why do you think geodesic domes are not popular as homes?

_____

_____

4 Would you want to live in a geodesic dome? Why or why not?

_____

_____

B. Discuss the questions and your answers with a partner.

Below are the key words you will practise in this chapter. Check the words you understand and then underline the words you use.

> These words are from the Longman Communication 3000 and the Academic Word List. See Appendix 2, page 158.

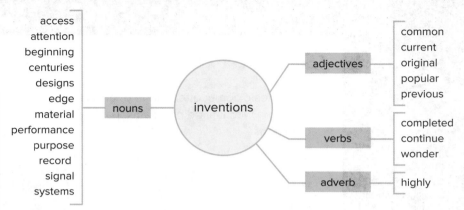

nouns:
- access
- attention
- beginning
- centuries
- designs
- edge
- material
- performance
- purpose
- record
- signal
- systems

inventions

adjectives:
- common
- current
- original
- popular
- previous

verbs:
- completed
- continue
- wonder

adverb:
- highly

FOCUS ON LISTENING

Listening for Main Points

When you listen, it is sometimes difficult to remember everything you hear. Instead, listen for main points: explanations of how or why something works and examples that make the idea easier to understand.

Listen for main points by identifying:

- what has happened or is happening—the main action of the sentence or paragraph;
- key words that are repeated and show who or what is important;
- answers to questions;
- ideas that usually come before examples or explanations.

> Key words are usually nouns and verbs, not adjectives, adverbs, or other parts of speech.

A. Listen to this excerpt from Listening 1. While you listen, underline the key words—words that are repeated. Highlight the main point.

> **EXCERPT 1**
>
> Daedalus went to Crete to work for King Minos. But, after Daedalus completed his work, the king said he would never let Daedalus leave. Daedalus needed to find a way to escape. Daedalus used wax and feathers to make wings for himself and his son, Icarus. Then they jumped out of a high window in the king's palace and flew away.

B. Listen to two other excerpts from Listening 1. While you listen, underline the key words—words that are repeated.

> **EXCERPT 2**
>
> **HELEN HARRIS:** I usually work with flying things. Though now I'm making kites, not wings.
>
> **CARL ROWAN:** Kites? Like kids' toys?
>
> **HARRIS:** Not quite. The kites provide Wi-Fi, high over villages. They are used in areas that don't have Internet connections. More than half the world doesn't have Wi-Fi or Internet access.

© ERPI • Reproduction prohibited

When you listen for main points, ignore questions and details.

EXCERPT 3

ROWAN: How does your Wi-Fi kite work?

HARRIS: Imagine a valley that frequently has strong winds, or at least strong winds part of the time. The kite has solar cells on it and a Wi-Fi transmitter. First, you fly it above the edge of the valley. Then the kite catches a signal. Last, it relays the signal to the valley and people can use the Internet on their laptops and phones.

C. Highlight the main point in Excerpt 3. Discuss with a partner.

FOCUS ON CRITICAL THINKING

Sketching What You Hear

Critical thinking is about trying to understand things in new ways. Converting what you hear into quick sketches can help you think about questions you should ask. You can also sketch things to help explain them. Follow these suggestions.

- Listen carefully and try to imagine what is being described. If the description is of a process, you can draw a diagram that shows steps.
- Draw a rough sketch—you don't have to be a famous artist!
- Compare your sketch with what you heard or what you want explained.
- Does your sketch make the description easy to understand? What does it not explain? What questions do you still have?

A. Read this excerpt from Listening 2. Underline the words or phrases that help you understand what the invention looks like. Then draw a sketch and share it with a partner.

The first invention is one by artificial intelligence pioneer, Marvin Minsky. It's commonly called "the useless machine." Inventions normally have a purpose, so you may wonder why it has that name. Let me show you. On the box is a toggle switch. First you flip the switch, and then, see, a little wooden finger comes out and flips the switch off. The machine is called the useless machine, but it always makes people laugh. Perhaps its true purpose is to entertain.

sketch

B. Do you still have questions about the useless machine? Write two.

- _____
- _____

© ERPI • Reproduction prohibited

LISTENING ❶ **High Flying Dreams**

In 1943, an engineer named Richard T. James (1914–1974) accidentally dropped an industrial spring and the spring continued to move. He thought it would make a good toy and, two years later, the first of 400 Slinky toys sold out in ninety minutes. Now, 250 million are sold every year. Some inventions use old ideas in new ways. What new uses could you find for a popular child's toy?

In the following exercises, explore key words from Listening 1.

A. Fill in the blanks with the correct words to complete the sentences.

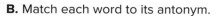

| access | beginning | common | completed | edge | signal |

1. Don't start at the end of the story, start at the _____.
2. On the mountain, our phones can't get a _____.
3. You need a password to get Wi-Fi _____.
4. I started my project late but _____ it on time.
5. Meeting new people is a _____ experience.
6. I like being on a high cliff, but I can't look over the _____.

B. Match each word to its antonym.

WORDS		ANTONYMS
1 beginning (n.)	_____	a) not started
2 common (adj.)	_____	b) old
3 completed (v.)	_____	c) ending
4 current (adj.)	_____	d) silence
5 signal (n.)	_____	e) unusual

C. What do the words in bold mean to you? Complete the sentences.

1. What is something you recently **completed**?

    I recently completed _____

2. What is a **common** thing you do every day?

    Every day, I _____

3. What is one of your **current** interests?

    One current interest is _____

4. How do you get Internet **access**?

    I get access _____

Before You Listen

A. Read this excerpt from Listening 1. Underline the main point.

> **CARL ROWAN:** Hello, and welcome *Invention Weekly Podcast* listeners! Today we have inventor Helen Harris in our studio. Helen, let's start at the beginning. Did you always want to be an inventor?
>
> **HELEN HARRIS:** Yes. I got interested in inventing because of the story of Daedalus.

© ERPI • Reproduction prohibited

B. Answer these questions. Then discuss with a partner.

① Who is Carl Rowan?

_____

② Who is Helen Harris?

_____

③ Who was Daedalus?

_____

④ What is the connection between Harris and Daedalus?

_____

C. Harris uses kites to provide Wi-Fi access. What do you think would be a problem with using kites to provide Wi-Fi? Write one idea and discuss it with your partner.

_____

_____

While You Listen

D. Listen the first time to understand the general idea. Read the sentences and phrases in the sections column and then listen to get the main point of each section. Listen again and take short notes. Then use your notes to write the main points in full.

SECTIONS	MAIN POINTS
❶ Hello, and welcome *Invention Weekly Podcast* listeners ... He was an inventor in a Greek myth.	*Harris got interested in inventing because of the story of Daedalus.*
❷ My school seldom taught Greek mythology ... jumped out of a high window in the king's palace and flew away.	*Daedalus needed to find a way to escape.*
❸ Now I remember this ... It's not often that a story makes someone want to become an inventor!	
❹ It was the *inventing* part—making something new out of common materials ... Finally, I jumped off a ladder.	
❺ How did that work for you ... the excitement of inventing stayed with me.	
❻ So, tell us about your current work ... More than half the world doesn't have Internet access.	
❼ How does your Wi-Fi kite work ... people can use the Internet on their laptops and phones.	
❽ Ah, I think I've heard something about this ... And please don't jump off any ladders!	

© ERPI • Reproduction prohibited

After You Listen

E. Number these main points in order to form an outline of Listening 1.
Then compare them with the main points you wrote in While You Listen.
Did you identify the same main points? Discuss with a partner.

_____ Harris got interested in inventing because of the story of Daedalus.

_____ Daedalus needed to find a way to escape.

_____ Harris broke her arm.

_____ Icarus fell into the sea and died.

_____ Kites are a cheap and local alternative.

_____ The kites provide Wi-Fi, high over villages.

_____ Harris made wings with feathers.

_____ The kite catches a signal.

F. Indicate whether these statements are true or false, according to the listening.

STATEMENTS		TRUE	FALSE
❶	Helen Harris is interviewed because she is an inventor.		
❷	The story of Daedalus shows how inventions can go wrong.		
❸	The story of jumping off a ladder showed Harris' early success.		
❹	Harris is using balloons to provide Wi-Fi to people in valleys.		
❺	Expensive options are usually best for poorer people.		
❻	A local alternative means people in the valley can control it.		

FOCUS ON GRAMMAR

Adverbs of Frequency

Adverbs modify verbs by describing how things happen. Adverbs of frequency have a special purpose. They help you or your listeners understand how often something happens.

Rough percentages let you see the frequency of events for each adverb.

0% ◄——————————————— 50% ————————————————► 100%

never   rarely   seldom   sometimes   often   usually   always

A. Complete these sentences. Discuss with a partner.

I never _____

I sometimes _____

I always _____

© ERPI • Reproduction prohibited

PLACEMENT OF ADVERBS OF FREQUENCY	EXAMPLES
before or after the verb	She **often** reads. She reads **often**.
after a form of the verb *be*	He is **usually** happy.
after the modal or auxiliary verb	He would **seldom** go there.
after the subject, in questions	Do they **always** study together?

B. Draw an arrow ↓ to indicate where the adverb in parentheses should be placed in each sentence.

1 (always) Did you↓want to be an inventor ?

2 (seldom) My school taught Greek mythology .

3 (never) The king said he would let Daedalus leave .

4 (often) It's not that a story makes someone want to become an inventor !

5 (usually) I work with flying things .

6 (frequently) Imagine a valley that has strong winds .

7 (rarely) Those sorts of projects are affordable .

Visit My eLab to complete Grammar Review exercises for this chapter.

LISTENING 2

The Useless Machine

There are different motivations for inventing new things. Some people invent to solve problems. Others do so to make money. Inventing new things requires a combination of skills. Inventors need curiosity, imagination, and technical skills to turn dreams into reality. Would you like to be an inventor?

VOCABULARY BUILD

In the following exercises, explore key words from Listening 2.

A. Fill in the blanks with the correct words to complete the sentences.

centuries	material	original	wonder

1 Plastic is a modern _____, only invented in 1907.

2 I _____ how Egyptians built the pyramids four thousand years ago.

3 The _____ zeppelin airships were first flown commercially in 1910.

4 Napoleon Bonaparte was born more than two _____ ago, in 1769.

© ERPI • Reproduction prohibited

B. *Collocations* are words typically used together. Often, collocations have particular meanings that you cannot guess just from knowing the words separately. Match each collocation to its meaning. Key words are in bold.

COLLOCATIONS		MEANINGS
❶ pay **attention**	_____	a) make something pointless
❷ stand at **attention**	_____	b) have a particular use
❸ defeat the **purpose**	_____	c) wanted by most people
❹ serve a **purpose**	_____	d) focus on something
❺ **popular** demand	_____	e) not what most people think
❻ contrary to **popular** belief	_____	f) remain upright, for a ceremony

C. What do the words in bold mean to you? Complete the sentences.

❶ What do you do to pay **attention**?

I pay attention by _____

❷ What is something you **wonder** about?

I wonder about _____

❸ What is something **original** that you do?

Something original I do _____

❹ What is a **popular** song you like?

I like _____

Before You Listen

A. Read this excerpt from Listening 2. Then choose the word or phrase that best completes each sentence.

> If I can have your attention, please. Thank you. Hello. I'm Dr. Dennis Baxter and I welcome you to the Science Museum. I would like to give a short talk about four inventions. Two of them are inventions we rarely hear about. After, I'd like you to discuss the inventions and let me know which one you like best and why.

❶ Dr. Dennis Baxter works _____.

a) as an inventor   b) at the Science Museum

❷ Dr. Baxter is going to talk about four _____.

a) inventions   b) inventors

❸ After, he wants the audience to _____.

a) make new inventions   b) discuss the inventions

❹ Listeners should explain why they like one _____.

a) the most   b) the least

© ERPI • Reproduction prohibited

B. One of the inventions is a hula hoop. Fill in the blanks to describe a hula hoop and to explain how to use it. Use adverbs of frequency when describing how often: *always, never, sometimes*. Share your description with a partner.

How to Use a Hula Hoop
A hula hoop is a plastic tube that is <u>*always*</u> in the shape of _____. You _____ put it around _____. You _____ stop moving or the hula hoop _____. Hula hoops are _____ used in exercise classes.

While You Listen

C. Listening 2 talks about four different inventions. You have already read about the first one, the useless machine, and the second one, the hula hoop. The first time you listen, take short notes, on a separate sheet of paper, on the main points of each invention. After you listen a second time, write your notes in sentences as main points in the table.

D. Listen a third time for sentences with adverbs of frequency. Write the adverbs in the blanks.

INVENTIONS	MAIN POINTS	ADVERBS OF FREQUENCY
INTRODUCTION	*I would like to give a short talk about inventions.*	Two of them are inventions we <u>*rarely*</u> hear about.
THE USELESS MACHINE		Inventions <u>*usually*</u> have a clear purpose. It _____ makes people laugh.
HULA HOOP		The second invention is something you _____ see kids play with—a hula hoop.
HAPPY FACE		The third invention is Bernard and Murray Spain's happy face, _____ seen with the slogan, "Have a nice day."
VIDEO DATING MACHINE		Of course, today, you _____ use your phone to have the same kind of video chat. So this is a case of a good idea that _____ worked at the time.

© **ERPI** • Reproduction prohibited

After You Listen

E. Match the inventions to the main points of the talk. Then check what you wrote in While You Listen. Do you have the same points? Discuss with a partner.

INVENTIONS		MAIN POINTS
❶ useless machine	_____	a) A new material—plastic—helped make an old invention more popular.
❷ hula hoop	_____	b) This invention wasn't original or made from new materials, but it was marketed—or sold—in a new way.
❸ happy face	_____	c) This is a case of a good idea that never worked at the time.
❹ video dating machine	_____	d) The machine sometimes makes people laugh.

F. Choose the best answer to each question.

❶ Why is the useless machine different from other inventions?

a) Other machines usually have a clear purpose.

b) Other machines don't make people laugh.

❷ Before plastic, what were hula hoops made from?

a) They were made from wood and metal.

b) They were made from wood or bamboo.

❸ How was the "have a nice day" slogan used?

a) It often went with the happy face image.

b) It replaced the happy face image.

❹ Why do you think the video dating machine didn't become popular?

a) Too many people wanted to use it.

b) It was not as convenient as meeting in person.

G. In the talk, Dr. Baxter says, "Inventors identify problems but sometimes have to wait for new technologies to solve them." Write three new materials or technologies that are making new inventions possible. Discuss with a partner.

_____

_____

H. Dr. Baxter asks his listeners to choose their favourite invention. Choose the one you like best. Explain why you like it and then discuss with a partner.

_____

_____

_____

_____

© **ERPI** • Reproduction prohibited

Using Linking Words

When you read, it is easy to follow a set of instructions or a sequence of events. You start at the top and go down a list. If you don't understand something, you can go back a step. But when you speak, your listeners need to be able to understand and remember each step or event. You can help them by linking the information with words that indicate sequence.

Common linking words include cardinal and ordinal numbers. Cardinal numbers include *one, two, three,* and ordinal numbers include *first, second, third.* These are sometimes used with other linking words like *then, next, last,* or *finally.*

A. Rewrite these sentences using linking words. Practise saying your answers with a partner.

1 I cut open two pillows. I glued the feathers onto pieces of cardboard. I jumped off a ladder.

_____

_____

_____

2 You fly it above the edge of the valley. It catches a signal from the ground. It relays the signal to the valley and people can use the Internet on their laptops and phones.

_____

_____

_____

_____

_____

B. Think of a simple task with four steps, like how to use a common tool. Use linking words to connect the steps.

- _____

_____

- _____

_____

- _____

_____

- _____

_____

Explaining steps are important for tasks such as giving directions.

© **ERPI** • Reproduction prohibited

FOCUS ON SPEAKING

WARM-UP ASSIGNMENT
Explain an Invention to a Partner

In this Warm-Up Assignment you will choose a simple invention and explain how it works to a partner. You will use this information to further discuss the invention in the Final Assignment.

A. Choose an invention. It can be something old or new, but it should require some steps to use it: for example, a Jenga tower of blocks and how to build the tower and remove blocks without it falling.

B. Draw a small sketch of the invention you chose (see Focus on Critical Thinking, page 25).

C. Write notes on how it works. Link the steps together with words that indicate sequence (see Focus on Speaking, previous page).

D. Use what you learned in Focus on Grammar (page 28) to add three points about what your invention *always* does, *sometimes* does, or *never* does.

E. Practise explaining your invention. Use your sketch, the linked steps, and adverbs of frequency.

F. Explain your invention to a partner. Ask for feedback on what you could improve.

Use feedback from your teacher and classmates on this Warm-Up Assignment to improve your speaking.

LISTENING ❸ | **Canadian Develops Futuristic Hoverboard**

When you dream, you may imagine you can fly. Flying has a sense of freedom, like being a bird. Alexandru Duru is a young inventor who lives in Montreal, Canada. He built a hoverboard that he can stand on and fly for a few minutes before the batteries run out. Perhaps in a few years you will be able to use one to take longer trips. Would you like to be able to fly?

VOCABULARY BUILD

In the following exercises, explore key words from Listening 3.

A. Match each word to its definition. Look up the words you don't know.

WORDS		DEFINITIONS
❶ continue (v.)	_____	a) show of some kind
❷ highly (adv.)	_____	b) sets of things working together
❸ performance (n.)	_____	c) happened before
❹ previous (adj.)	_____	d) go on
❺ systems (n.)	_____	e) above average level or degree

© **ERPI** • Reproduction prohibited

Pronunciation: When "record" is a noun, stress the first syllable. When it's a verb, stress the second syllable. Stress the second syllable of "designs" whether it's a noun or verb.

My eLab 🖉

Visit My eLab to complete a pronunciation exercise.

Visit My eLab to complete Vocabulary Review exercises for this chapter.

B. The words *record* and *designs* can be used as nouns or verbs with different pronunciations. Complete the sentences with the noun or verb forms of *record* and *designs*. Then practise saying the sentences.

1 She has a new job where she _____ packages for tea.

2 We watched the runner from Kenya break a world _____.

3 Could you _____ the lecture? I can't be there today.

4 We looked at three _____ for posters and chose one.

C. What do the words in bold mean to you? Complete the sentences.

1 What **design** do you like in clothes?

I like _____

2 What is your favourite kind of **performance**?

My favourite kind of performance _____

3 What **previous** interest do you no longer have?

I'm no longer interested in _____

4 What is something you will **continue** to do after you graduate?

I will continue to _____

Before You Listen

A. Read this excerpt from Listening 3. Some of the words are technical and difficult to understand. Underline the information that is the most important.

> **REG SHERREN:** In an older, industrial section of Montreal, you can find Alexandru Duru working away in his shop amongst the clutter and the dirty dishes, and the list of things he's working on.
> This is what you do when you doodle?
> **ALEXANDRU DURU:** Yeah. Some discussions, part of a—remaining part of a to-do list, and some discussion of pulse width modulation, and engine motor controls.
> **SHERREN:** There's a machine carving 3D engine designs in the corner. Computers and parts stacked up everywhere.

B. Now choose the main point of the excerpt.

☐ You can find Alexandru Duru working away in his shop amongst the clutter.

☐ This is what you do when you doodle?

☐ Some discussion of pulse width modulation and engine motor controls.

☐ Computers and parts stacked up everywhere.

C. Alexandru Duru has invented a hoverboard that he can fly on. Indicate which challenges you think he had to face.

☐ lack of interest from others

☐ batteries that last long enough

☐ finding someone to fly the hoverboard

☐ safety issues

While You Listen

D. Listening 3 explains Alexandru Duru's invention. Listen the first time to understand the general idea. Then read the sections and the sample main points. While you listen a second time, write notes about the main point of each section. Listen a third time to fill in details.

SECTIONS	MAIN POINTS
1 In an older, industrial section of Montreal ... Pretty much, yeah.	*You can find Alexandru Duru working away in his shop amongst the clutter.*
2 He has a company now, Omni Hoverboards Inc. ... can make a human fly.	*He has a company now, Omni Hoverboards Inc.*
3 So what, did you have a dream—I'm going to fly ... Why not?	
4 As a boy, after his family emigrated from Romania ... this has been the obsession.	
5 Oh yeah, that's light ... you control it with your feet, with your hands?	
6 His design is a little different ... Yeah, you would want that.	*His design is a little different (uses pliers).*
7 And batteries ... And then—	*One and a half minutes (time to shatter the world record).*
8 But that was all it took ... And you've heard from around the world.	
9 But he's not slowing down ... The magic of flight that has captured our imaginations since Orville and Wilbur Wright.	

After You Listen

E. Check your answers in Before You Listen, task C. Were you correct? Discuss with a partner.

F. Use your notes to help you number the main points of Listening 3 in order.

_____ You can find Alexandru Duru working away in his shop amongst the clutter.

_____ He flew for almost 300 metres, watched by six and a half million people.

_____ He designed this 3D imaging technology.

_____ He has a company now, Omni Hoverboards Inc.

_____ His design is a little different (uses pliers).

_____ It's a combination of carbon and high-tech electronics.

_____ It took one and a half minutes to shatter the world record.

_____ You could make something like that today.

_____ He designs his highly secretive next generation hoverboard.

© ERPI • Reproduction prohibited

G. Choose the word or phrase that best completes each sentence.

1. The problem with Duru's early hoverboard was that it _____.
   a) caught fire
   b) didn't float
   c) fell over

2. The time of one and a half minutes was important because _____.
   a) few people flew for longer times
   b) it meant short trips were possible
   c) it broke a world record

3. Duru realized that a hoverboard was possible because _____.
   a) of new technology
   b) his father could help
   c) everyone likes to fly

4. Duru worked at the Metropolitan Opera House in New York as _____.
   a) a performer
   b) a software engineer
   c) an inventor

Alexandru Duru

5. Duru has been obsessed with making a hoverboard for the past _____.
   a) few months
   b) few years
   c) year

6. Duru's plan is to _____.
   a) make secret surfboards
   b) go back to university to study
   c) make a better hoverboard

7. The phrase "parts come from all over the world" suggests _____.
   a) Duru likes to shop everywhere
   b) Duru doesn't know how to shop
   c) the parts are not easy to find

8. The fact that Duru's father was an electrical engineer probably means _____.
   a) Duru could learn a lot from him
   b) his father competed with him
   c) Duru had no choice for his job

© ERPI • Reproduction prohibited

Discussing a New Topic

When you give a presentation, you may introduce a new topic for discussion. When you discuss the new topic, you need to keep the interest of your listeners and make sure they understand.

One technique is a) to tell them what you will tell them, b) tell them, and c) tell them what you told them. The idea is you introduce your topic, explain it, and then summarize it at the end. This repetition makes your topic easier to remember.

A. Compare these two paragraphs. Which is more effective? Why?

PARAGRAPH 1	PARAGRAPH 2
Bernard and Murray Spain didn't invent the image themselves; the brothers just bought the rights. Then they put it on every product they could. Within eighteen months, they had made $50 million.	Let me tell you about the success of the happy face image. Bernard and Murray Spain didn't invent the image themselves; the brothers just bought the rights. Then they put it on every product they could. Within eighteen months, they had made $50 million. Making a lot of money in a short time is the dream of many business people.

_____

_____

B. After you present your topic, check your listeners' understanding by asking questions. Write two questions you could ask about the information in paragraph 2. Use *who, what, when, where, why,* or *how* to start your questions.

• _____

• _____

C. Write answers to the questions in task B and practise them with a partner. If the information is not available, say, "I don't know" or "I'm not sure."

• _____

• _____

© ERPI • Reproduction prohibited

FINAL ASSIGNMENT

Discuss an Invention with a Partner

Use what you learned in this chapter to discuss an invention with a partner.

A. Begin with your explanation of the invention you chose in the Warm-Up Assignment (page 34).

B. Based on the feedback you received, consider how you can improve the description of the invention.

C. Use the steps from Academic Survival Skill to structure your discussion with your partner. Write notes in the table.

STEPS	NOTES
❶ Introduce what you will talk about. Present your sketch of the invention you chose.	
❷ Use linking words to explain what the invention does. Summarize the information.	
❸ Ask a question to make sure your partner understands. Invite your partner to ask questions about the invention.	

D. Ask for feedback about your discussion so you can improve next time.

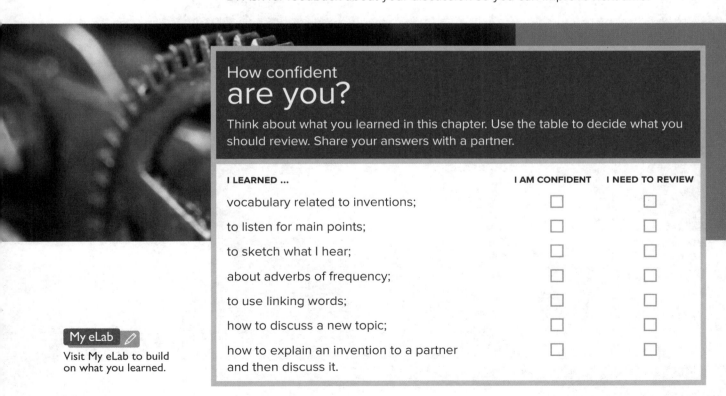

How confident are you?

Think about what you learned in this chapter. Use the table to decide what you should review. Share your answers with a partner.

I LEARNED ...	I AM CONFIDENT	I NEED TO REVIEW
vocabulary related to inventions;	☐	☐
to listen for main points;	☐	☐
to sketch what I hear;	☐	☐
about adverbs of frequency;	☐	☐
to use linking words;	☐	☐
how to discuss a new topic;	☐	☐
how to explain an invention to a partner and then discuss it.	☐	☐

My eLab ✎

Visit My eLab to build on what you learned.

CHAPTER 3

The Sharing Economy

Many people own things they don't need or seldom use. For example, most cars are unused 92 percent of the time. Rooms, tools, and skills may be underused. The sharing economy provides opportunities to avoid wasting resources and to make money. A sharing economy can also help reduce waste and improve communities. A few individuals have become enormously wealthy through the sharing economy. Some barely make enough to live, while others don't care. What things and skills could you share?

In this chapter, you will

- learn vocabulary related to the sharing economy;
- listen for specific details;
- question assumptions;
- review count and non-count nouns;
- use talking points;
- use mind maps to take notes;
- examine and present a sharing economy business.

GEARING UP

A. Look at the infographic and then answer the questions.

Aspects of the Sharing Economy

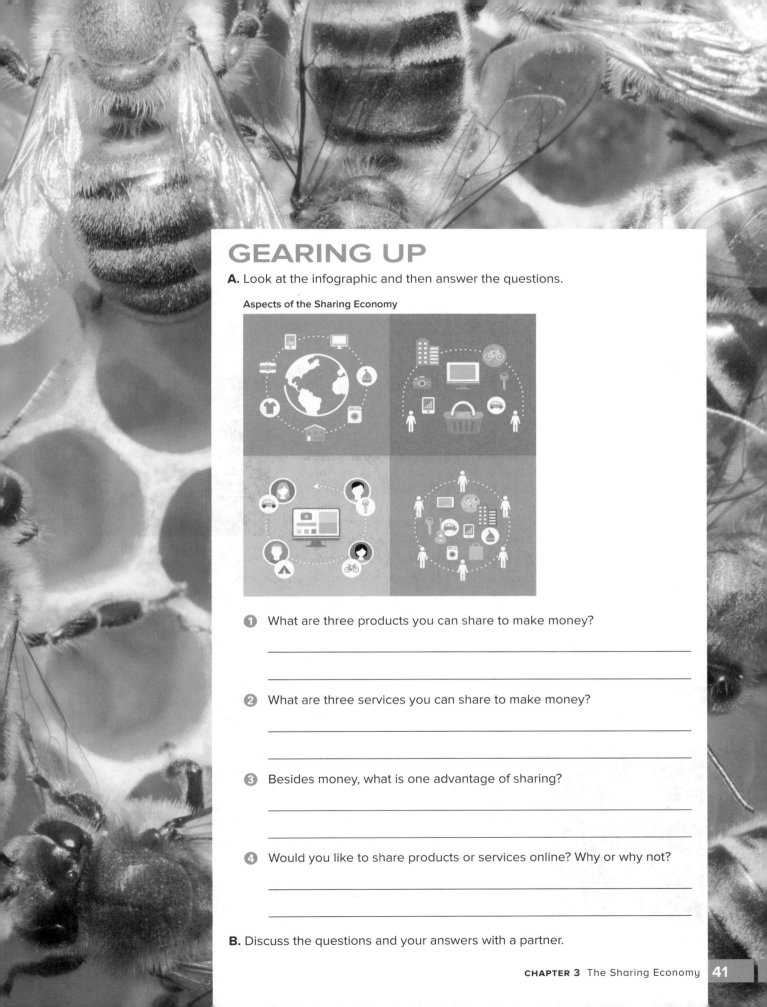

1 What are three products you can share to make money?

_____

_____

2 What are three services you can share to make money?

_____

_____

3 Besides money, what is one advantage of sharing?

_____

_____

4 Would you like to share products or services online? Why or why not?

_____

_____

B. Discuss the questions and your answers with a partner.

Below are the key words you will practise in this chapter. Check the words you understand and then underline the words you use.

These words are from the Longman Communication 3000 and the Academic Word List. See Appendix 2, page 158.

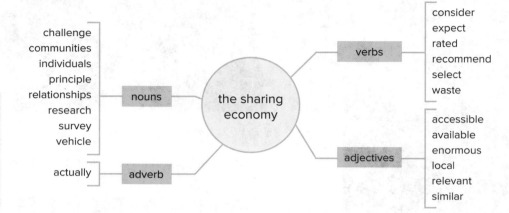

nouns: challenge, communities, individuals, principle, relationships, research, survey, vehicle

adverb: actually

the sharing economy

verbs: consider, expect, rated, recommend, select, waste

adjectives: accessible, available, enormous, local, relevant, similar

---

FOCUS ON LISTENING

Listening for Specific Details

At an airport, you hear hundreds of announcements. But you are probably only interested in information about your flight. In this case, you listen for *specific details,* such as your flight number. You want to answer the question: When is my flight? Once you know the question, you will know which key words to listen for. Follow this advice when listening for specific details.

• Think of a question about what information is important.

• Listen for phrases such as *for example* or *for instance.*

• Listen for key words, such as numbers, related to your question.

A. This excerpt from Listening 1 talks about three factors. The number *three* is a clue that you should listen for something specific. Underline the specific details that are important.

Visit My eLab to learn more about numbers.

> I'd like to introduce three factors that help make the modern sharing economy possible: social media, online banking, and smart phones.

B. Listen to an excerpt from Listening 2. It has four numbers. The first time you listen, write the numbers. Listen again and write what each number represents. Then compare your answers with a partner.

NUMBERS	REPRESENTS
60,000,000	

© **ERPI** • Reproduction prohibited

C. The title of Listening 3 is "AskforTask CEO Interview." CEO stands for *Chief Executive Officer*. AskforTask is a service that connects people who have tasks to do with people who can help. Write *wh-* questions to get specific information about the app. Practise your questions with a partner.

1 Who *is the CEO?* _____

2 What _____

3 When *was the service invented?* _____

4 Where _____

5 Why *was it invented?* _____

6 How _____

FOCUS ON CRITICAL THINKING

Questioning Assumptions

An assumption is something you take as true without proof. When you listen, identify and question your assumptions and try to see the potential problems or flaws in them. Consider this excerpt from Listening 1.

> Fifth, is that the sharing economy builds stronger communities. Sophie may find she's good at painting apartments. She decides to use borrowed tools to help other people paint their apartments. She may trade her painting services, trading apartment painting for a farmer's fruit and vegetables. In doing so, she meets and gets to know people with similar interests.

The idea is that Sophie helps build stronger communities by trading services for goods. The assumption is that this is practical (easy to do) and good (benefits everyone). But if you question these two assumptions you may see some problems.

A. Read each problem with the sharing economy and indicate whether this means it is not practical for Sophie or not good for the community. Discuss with a partner.

PROBLEMS	NOT PRACTICAL FOR SOPHIE	NOT GOOD FOR THE COMMUNITY
1 Sophie and the farmer need to spend a lot of time to organize a trade.		
2 Sophie and the farmer may not pay taxes when they trade so there is less money for things like public schools.		
3 The farmer only grows corn; Sophie can't use hundreds of dollars worth of corn.		
4 Sophie and the farmer don't build a relationship because, after the job is done, they have no reason to meet.		

B. Think of one other topic that you assume is true: for example, *recycling is good*. Discuss your assumption with a partner and try to identify potential problems, such as recycling might be costly and ineffective.

© **ERPI** • Reproduction prohibited

 **Conditions and Benefits of the Modern Sharing Economy**

Three factors make the modern sharing economy possible: social media, online banking, and smart phones. In Listening 1, Dr. Amy Chow explains how these work together. She also talks about five benefits. Are you part of the sharing economy?

VOCABULARY BUILD

In the following exercises, explore key words from Listening 1.

A. Match each word to its synonym. Use a dictionary to look up those you don't know.

WORDS		SYNONYMS
❶ accessible (adj.)	_____	a) connections
❷ consider (v.)	_____	b) available
❸ relationships (n.)	_____	c) think about
❹ relevant (adj.)	_____	d) important

❗ Vocabulary Tip: When you learn new words, learn their synonyms as well.

B. Fill in the blanks with the correct words to complete the paragraph.

communities	consider	individuals	similar

We need to _____ people who live in _____ outside of cities. They may not have access to online banking or _____ services. These _____ probably did not have smart phones a few decades ago and used mail for most messages. But they now want to bank and shop online.

C. What do the words in bold mean to you? Complete the sentences.

❶ What do you **consider** to be your best quality?

My best quality is _____

❷ What is something you and your friends do that is **similar**?

Something similar we do _____

❸ What is a **community** you belong to?

One community I belong to _____

❹ What is your most **relevant** subject in college?

My most relevant subject is _____

Before You Listen

A. What do you know about social media, online banking, and smart phones? Do you use them all? How do you use them? Discuss with a partner.

© ERPI • Reproduction prohibited

B. Read this excerpt from Listening 1. Underline specific details about what you can share. Highlight specific details about things you can do.

> Let's start with social media. As I'm sure you know, social media is all about sharing. You likely share information in the form of text, pictures, video, and so on. To paraphrase Murthy, writing in 2013, social media refers to relatively inexpensive and widely accessible digital tools. He says they allow individuals to publish and access information. Users can also collaborate on common causes and build relationships.

While You Listen

C. The first time you listen, try to understand the general idea. The second time, listen for specific details and fill in the missing information in the tables. Listen a third time to check the details.

FACTORS	SPECIFIC DETAILS	
	NAMES OF COMPANIES	WHAT THE COMPANIES DO
SOCIAL MEDIA	*eBay*	*connects customers with relevant products and services*
ONLINE BANKING		*ships goods internationally / trust you will be paid*
SMART PHONES	Uber	

BENEFITS	SPECIFIC DETAILS	
	EXAMPLES	EXPLANATIONS
❶ save money	*doesn't buy things she doesn't need*	*some things you need only once*
❷ access goods		
❸ sustainability		*save raw materials*
❹ independence	*doing jobs on her own*	
❺ build communities	*bartering*	

After You Listen

D. These points are about the first part of Dr. Chow's talk, before the five key benefits. Number them in the correct order to form a summary.

_____ The modern sharing economy has three factors: social media, online banking, smart phones.

_____ In 1995, eBay offered online auctions and shopping.

_____ Social media refers to inexpensive and accessible digital tools.

_____ Online payment systems let you know you will be paid.

_____ Search tools make it easy to find what you need.

_____ Social media includes sharing text, pictures, and video.

_____ Smart phones are used to locate nearby Uber drivers.

_____ This model of the sharing economy was not possible twenty years ago.

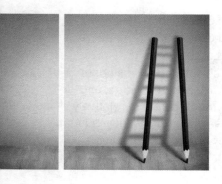

E. Connect the phrases to summarize the second part of Listening 1 on the five benefits.

SUMMARY		
❶ People who share pay less ...	_____	a) you don't have to store things.
❷ You can save money if you don't ...	_____	b) save money by not hiring people.
❸ Sharing also saves space because ...	_____	c) than when they buy things.
❹ Sharing means less production and ...	_____	d) people sharing and working together.
❺ By doing things on your own, you ...	_____	e) the use of fewer raw materials.
❻ Communities are built by ...	_____	f) have to repair things.

F. Read the following assumptions. Question each assumption. Write notes and then discuss with a partner.

ASSUMPTIONS	QUESTIONS
❶ Buying and selling on eBay is easy for everyone.	
❷ PayPal makes people trust online banking.	
❸ Getting a ride with Uber benefits everyone.	

FOCUS ON GRAMMAR

Count and Non-Count Nouns

Some nouns can be counted and some cannot. Count nouns are things like *bottles*. Non-count nouns are things like *water*. When you listen, knowing if something is a count noun or a non-count noun helps you better understand the topic. Besides learning common count and non-count nouns, you can also spot them in these ways:

• Count nouns are often paired with the articles *a* or *an*: **a** laptop, **an** elephant.

• Count nouns use *many* to express quantity: I have **many** books.

• Non-count nouns do not have a plural form.

• Non-count nouns use *much* to express quantity: There is too **much** rain today.

© **ERPI** • Reproduction prohibited

A. Indicate whether the words in bold are count or non-count nouns.

SENTENCES	COUNT	NON-COUNT
1 Maybe Airbnb hurts the hotel **industry**.		
2 Are you hearing any bad **news** about this?		
3 She wanted to have some **fun**.		
4 Use my apartment for a short **vacation**.		
5 Hosts earn extra **money**.		
6 You get a **code** and use the car for a short trip.		
7 There are many **alternatives** to Craigslist.		
8 Craigslist is getting a lot of **traffic**.		

B. Complete these sentences. Choose the word in parentheses that best describes the count or non-count noun.

1 The bus ticket didn't cost (many / much) money.

2 She has (many / much) friends at school.

3 I don't drink (many / much) coffee anymore.

4 How (many / much) people will come to the meeting?

5 Were (many / much) computers free at the lab?

6 I'm sorry, but I don't have (many / much) time.

7 How (much / many) things in your home do you use less than once a month?

8 Let's see how (much / many) time we have.

My eLab
Visit My eLab to complete Grammar Review exercises for this chapter.

LISTENING ❷   **Two Case Studies: Zipcar and Airbnb**

Two sharing economy success stories are Zipcar (a car rental business) and Airbnb (a home rental business). Zipcar shares its own cars. Airbnb's website connects guests to people's spare rooms, apartments, or houses. The two business models have social media in common. Why would you rent a Zipcar or an Airbnb room rather than getting a car from a traditional car rental business or renting a hotel room?

© ERPI • Reproduction prohibited

VOCABULARY
BUILD

In the following exercises, explore key words from Listening 2.

A. Fill in the blanks with the correct words to complete the sentences.

principle	survey	vehicle	waste

1. A bank may use a _____ to see if customers are satisfied.

2. Don't _____ things by buying more than you need.

3. The most important _____ of social media is sharing.

4. The only _____ she owns is a big truck.

B. Match each word to its definition.

WORDS		DEFINITIONS
❶ available (adj.)	_____	a) investigation into something
❷ enormous (adj.)	_____	b) not busy with something else
❸ research (n.)	_____	c) very large in size

C. What do the words in bold mean to you? Complete the sentences.

1. When are you usually **available** to meet friends?

   I'm usually available _____

2. What kind of **vehicle** would you like to drive?

   I'd like to drive _____

3. What product **research** would you do before buying something expensive?

   I'd research _____

4. What is something you sometimes **waste**?

   I sometimes waste _____

Before You Listen

A. Read this excerpt on how Airbnb began. What makes the last sentence of the paragraph so surprising? Discuss with a partner.

> In 2008, two friends invited three travellers to stay with them as an informal bed and breakfast, or B and B. There were no extra beds, so the friends gave them air mattresses. It started a billion dollar business.

B. Write three assumptions about Airbnb. For example, you may think it's a good way to make money. Discuss your assumptions in a group.

- _____

- _____

- _____

© ERPI • Reproduction prohibited

Visit My eLab to complete a pronunciation exercise.

Pronunciation: Listen carefully to numbers. Dates and times can be pronounced in different ways.

While You Listen

C. The first time you listen, try to understand the general idea. The second time, listen for numbers and write them in order. You will hear percentages, dates, and sums of money.

1 _80 percent_ _____

2 _____

3 _____

4 _____

5 _____

6 _____

7 _____

8 _____

9 _____

10 _US $_ _____

11 _72 percent_ _____

D. Listen again for specific details. Fill in the blanks to complete the statements.

1 People who use Zipcars are less likely to _____ an old car or to _____ a new one.

2 Zipcars led to 33,000 _____ vehicles on the road.

3 _____ began in 2008.

4 In 2015, Airbnb was in 57,000 _____ in 192 _____.

5 Hosts earn extra money: an average of US $7,000 a _____.

6 In New York, 72 percent of hosts use the money to pay for their own _____.

After You Listen

E. Connect the phrases to summarize the first part of Listening 2.

SUMMARY		
1 We buy things ...	_____	a) will reduce wasting.
2 Research shows that most people use 80 percent of the things ...	_____	b) to organize bicycle sharing.
3 It might be hard ...	_____	c) 20 percent delayed buying a new one.
4 People think a sharing economy ...	_____	d) often dropped off at different locations.
5 Statistical data about people using shared goods and services ...	_____	e) in their homes less than once a month.
6 Zipcars are booked online for short trips and ...	_____	f) and make the world greener.
7 Twenty percent of Zipcar users sold a vehicle and ...	_____	g) we don't need.
8 Sharing can reduce production and consumption ...	_____	h) looks encouraging.

F. Indicate whether these statements are important to Zipcar, to Airbnb, or to both. Then discuss your answers with a partner.

THIS BUSINESS IS GOOD ...	ZIPCAR	AIRBNB	BOTH
❶ if you travel to other cities.			
❷ if you don't like expensive hotels.			
❸ if don't have a lot of money.			
❹ if you seldom drive.			
❺ if you don't care about regulations.			
❻ if you're not worried about theft.			

FOCUS ON SPEAKING

Using Talking Points

Talking points can help you prepare for a presentation or discussion. They also help you focus on your topic. Usually, you write talking points as short notes on a page. But don't read them when you talk. Instead, learn the points or look at them briefly if you have to. Follow these steps:

- Identify your topic or the goal of your presentation or discussion. For example, your goal might be to introduce a new company.
- Think about questions your listeners might want answered about the topic: ask information questions.
- Write brief answers. You don't need to write in full sentences, just the main points.
- Practise saying your points.

> ❗ It's easier for people to remember three points. If you have many points, pick the best three.

A. One new sharing economy business is DogVacay. It tries to avoid the inconvenience to friends and family or the expense of professionals for taking care of your dog. Write three information questions you have about DogVacay. Share your questions with a partner.

- _____
- _____
- _____

B. Here is some information about DogVacay. Underline important talking points.

> It's hard to find someone to care for your dog when you're away. DogVacay's team finds the best people to watch your pet. Every sitter goes through an approval process. Customers review all our sitters. This helps you find the perfect match for you and your pet. Your pet's safety is really important to us. Every reservation includes customer support, daily photos, and insurance.

C. Choose three important points and practise talking about them. Use your talking points to explain DogVacay to a partner.

© **ERPI** • Reproduction prohibited

WARM-UP ASSIGNMENT
Examine a Sharing Economy Business

In this Warm-Up Assignment, you will choose a sharing economy business and learn more about it. Then you will describe the business to a partner.

A. Choose the sharing economy business you want to talk about. It could be one of the following or another one that you use.

- ☐ Craigslist (sells used goods)
- ☐ Gobble (delivers dinner)
- ☐ Kickstarter (funds projects)
- ☐ Lyft (shares cars)
- ☐ Skillshare (teaches skills)
- ☐ Smarter Parking (finds parking places)
- ☐ The Clothing Exchange (trades clothing)
- ☐ Other _____

B. Answer these questions about the business you chose. Look up answers on the Internet to questions you don't know.

QUESTIONS	ANSWERS
1 What does the business do?	
2 Who started the business?	
3 When did the business start?	
4 Where is the business located?	
5 Why is the business' product or service important?	
6 How does the business work?	

> ❶ *Use feedback from your teacher and classmates on this Warm-Up Assignment to improve your speaking.*

C. Add more information to your answers to make them more interesting. Try to use count and non-count nouns in your description of the business' product or service. (See Focus on Grammar, page 46.)

D. Use your answers to describe your sharing economy business to a partner. Ask for feedback on what you could do better.

© ERPI • Reproduction prohibited

Academic
Survival Skill

Using Mind Maps to Take Notes

Mind maps are based on the way you think. They are a useful note-taking tool. Mind maps can help you record what you hear and read.

A. Read this paragraph about the sharing economy. Highlight the main point and then underline specific details that are important to understanding the topic. (The blue text relates to task B.)

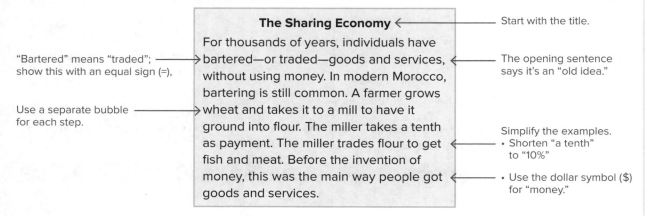

"Bartered" means "traded"; show this with an equal sign (=),

Use a separate bubble for each step.

The Sharing Economy ← Start with the title.

For thousands of years, individuals have bartered—or traded—goods and services, without using money. In modern Morocco, bartering is still common. A farmer grows wheat and takes it to a mill to have it ground into flour. The miller takes a tenth as payment. The miller trades flour to get fish and meat. Before the invention of money, this was the main way people got goods and services.

The opening sentence says it's an "old idea."

Simplify the examples.
• Shorten "a tenth" to "10%"
• Use the dollar symbol ($) for "money."

B. A mind map for the above paragraph might look like this. Use the blue text in task A to help you decide what has been left out. Discuss with a partner.

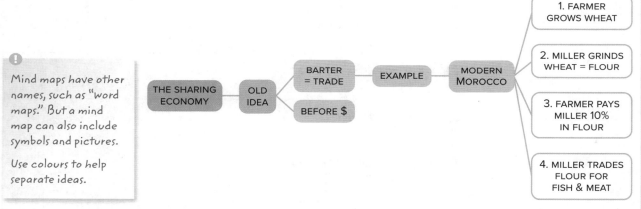

Mind maps have other names, such as "word maps." But a mind map can also include symbols and pictures.

Use colours to help separate ideas.

THE SHARING ECONOMY — OLD IDEA — BARTER = TRADE — EXAMPLE — MODERN MOROCCO
BEFORE $

1. FARMER GROWS WHEAT
2. MILLER GRINDS WHEAT = FLOUR
3. FARMER PAYS MILLER 10% IN FLOUR
4. MILLER TRADES FLOUR FOR FISH & MEAT

C. Speed up your note taking and simplify your mind map by using the following symbols. Add one more symbol and its meaning to the last row.

SYMBOLS	MEANINGS
!	important or surprising
=	equal
+	plus or and
−	minus or take away
@	at

SYMBOLS	MEANINGS
#	number
&	and
>	more than
<	less than

© **ERPI** • Reproduction prohibited

© ERPI • Reproduction prohibited

LISTENING ③ AskforTask CEO Interview

Some accidents lead to good things. Muneeb Mushtaq's mother had a problem in her kitchen that led Mushtaq to search for a plumber—someone who installs and repairs water pipes and fixtures. It was not a happy experience, but there was no way for Mushtaq to complain. It made him look for a new way to deal with small tasks.

VOCABULARY BUILD

In the following exercises, explore key words from Listening 3.

A. Fill in the blanks with the correct words to complete the paragraph.

challenge	expect	local	recommend	select

You never _____ an accident to happen but, when one does,

it can be a _____. For example, my car stopped working.

I needed to find someone _____ to fix it but didn't want to

_____ someone I didn't know. I asked a few friends if they

could _____ someone. They gave me a name of a mechanic

and she came and took care of my problem. Now we're friends!

B. Read the sentences. Then write the part of speech (adjective, adverb, noun, or verb) and the definition of the words in bold. Look up words you don't know in a dictionary.

SENTENCES	PARTS OF SPEECH	DEFINITIONS
❶ I wasn't sure, but he's **actually** delivering the package today.	*adverb*	*in fact, or really*
❷ When you face a **challenge** you get stronger when you meet it.		
❸ We like the **local** grocery store because it's more convenient.		
❹ My book club **rated** the twelve novels and chose our favourite one.		

C. What do the words in bold mean to you? Complete the sentences.

   ❶ What do you **expect** to do this weekend?

      I expect to _____

2 What is one big **challenge** in your life?

One challenge is _____

_____

3 Which movie would you **recommend** to a friend?

I would recommend _____

4 Which **local** food do you like to eat?

I like to eat _____

5 How do you **select** the books you read?

I usually _____

_____

My eLab 🖉

Visit My eLab to complete Vocabulary Review exercises for this chapter.

Before You Listen

A. Look at the photo. Write three small jobs in your home that you would like someone to help you with.

• _____

• _____

• _____

B. In Listening 3, Muneeb Mushtaq talks about how he came up with the idea for AskforTask, a service to find help for your small tasks. But people do not always talk in complete sentences and it can be difficult to listen for specific details. Read this paragraph and focus on the specific details. Then match the questions to the answers in the table that follows.

> Almost two years ago, my mom was washing dishes in the kitchen and broke the faucet. She asked me to find a plumber. On Craigslist I saw listings for plumbers but not prices or reviews. I chose one plumber. The plumber cost three times as what I thought and did a poor job. I wanted to leave a review but couldn't. I didn't want anyone else to go through that, so we created a platform that was more local and trustworthy.

QUESTIONS		ANSWERS
1 What was the problem that Mushtaq's mother faced?	_____	a) He looked for a plumber on Craigslist.
2 How did Mushtaq try to solve the problem?	_____	b) He charged too much and didn't do a good job.
3 Why was he unhappy with Craigslist?	_____	c) Her kitchen faucet broke.
4 Why was he unhappy with the plumber?	_____	d) It is more local and trustworthy.
5 What is different about Mushtaq's platform (online service)?	_____	e) He couldn't find prices or reviews.

© ERPI • Reproduction prohibited

C. Here is a mind map that summarizes some of the questions in Listening 3. There are answers to the first question. Read the questions with a partner and write any answers you can guess on a separate page.

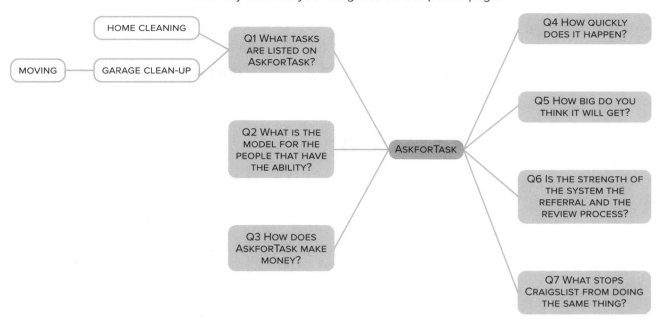

- HOME CLEANING
- MOVING — GARAGE CLEAN-UP

Q1 WHAT TASKS ARE LISTED ON ASKFORTASK?

Q2 WHAT IS THE MODEL FOR THE PEOPLE THAT HAVE THE ABILITY?

Q3 HOW DOES ASKFORTASK MAKE MONEY?

ASKFORTASK

Q4 HOW QUICKLY DOES IT HAPPEN?

Q5 HOW BIG DO YOU THINK IT WILL GET?

Q6 IS THE STRENGTH OF THE SYSTEM THE REFERRAL AND THE REVIEW PROCESS?

Q7 WHAT STOPS CRAIGSLIST FROM DOING THE SAME THING?

While You Listen

D. The first time you listen, try to understand the general idea. Before you listen a second time, read the questions. Then listen for details and take notes. Listen a third time to check your notes and add any details you might have missed.

QUESTIONS	ANSWERS
1 What tasks are listed on AskforTask?	*home cleaning* *garage clean-up* *moving*
2 What is the model for the people that have the ability?	taskers create profiles taskers list _____ and special interests
3 How does AskforTask make money?	
4 How quickly does it happen?	
5 How big do you think it will get?	not answered, but there are thirty-five _____ Canadians
6 Is the strength of the system the referral and the review process?	
7 What stops Craigslist from doing the same thing?	

After You Listen

E. Compare the answers you and your partner wrote in Before You Listen, task C. Were some answers the same as in Listening 3? Discuss what you would change with a partner.

F. Write answers to these information questions. Then discuss with a partner.

QUESTIONS	ANSWERS
1 Who is Muneeb Mushtaq?	*Muneeb Mushtaq is the founder and CEO of AskforTask.*
2 What does AskforTask do?	
3 When did Mushtaq start AskforTask?	
4 Where does AskforTask operate?	
5 Why do people use AskforTask?	
6 How do taskers (people who do the tasks) start working for AskforTask?	

FINAL ASSIGNMENT
Present a Sharing Economy Business

Use what you learned in this chapter to present your sharing economy business and answer questions about it.

A. Begin with your answers on the sharing economy business you chose in the Warm-Up Assignment (page 51). Turn your answers into talking points (see Focus on Speaking, page 50). Follow the structure in the table below.

STRUCTURE	TALKING POINTS
[name of the business] makes/helps/connects ...	
The business was started by ...	
The business was started in ...	

© ERPI • Reproduction prohibited

STRUCTURE	TALKING POINTS
The business is located at …	
The business' [product / service] is important because …	
The business …	

B. Based on the feedback you received, consider how you can improve your presentation.

C. Plan your presentation. Think of questions you might be asked and prepare answers.

D. Present your sharing economy business to a small group. Then answer questions that your classmates ask you.

E. While you listen to other students' presentations, take notes using the Academic Survival Skill mind map technique (page 52). Think of questions to ask.

F. Reflect on your presentation. Were you able to answer questions? What could you do better next time?

How confident are you?

Think about what you learned in this chapter. Use the table to decide what you should review. Share your answers with a partner.

I LEARNED …	I AM CONFIDENT	I NEED TO REVIEW
vocabulary related to the sharing economy;	☐	☐
to listen for specific details;	☐	☐
to question assumptions;	☐	☐
about count and non-count nouns;	☐	☐
to use talking points;	☐	☐
to use mind maps to take notes;	☐	☐
to examine and present a sharing economy business.	☐	☐

My eLab ✎
Visit My eLab to build on what you learned.

CHAPTER 4

Your Dream Job

Have you thought about your dream job? A dream job does not have to be one that pays the most money or one that makes you famous. There are other qualities that make a job enjoyable and rewarding. For example, many people want jobs where they do something that is meaningful and creative. They want to work with interesting people. They want to be challenged to solve problems. What qualities do you look for in your dream job?

In this chapter, you will

- learn vocabulary related to jobs;
- listen to compare;
- recognize point of view;
- review prepositions of time and place;
- disagree politely;
- learn how to work with a partner;
- describe your dream job and compare two jobs.

GEARING UP

A. Look at this bar chart of British people's most desirable jobs. Then answer the questions.

Britain's Most Desirable Jobs

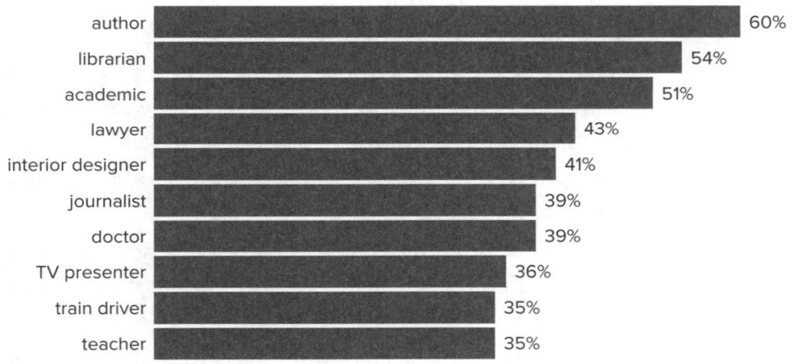

Job	Percentage
author	60%
librarian	54%
academic	51%
lawyer	43%
interior designer	41%
journalist	39%
doctor	39%
TV presenter	36%
train driver	35%
teacher	35%

① Which job on the chart would you most like to have? Why?

_____

_____

② Why might most people want to be an author?

_____

_____

③ Which job on the chart would you least like to have? Why?

_____

_____

④ Which job on the chart requires the most training? Which job requires the least?

_____

_____

B. Discuss the questions and your answers with a partner.

Below are the key words you will practise in this chapter. Check the words you understand and then underline the words you use.

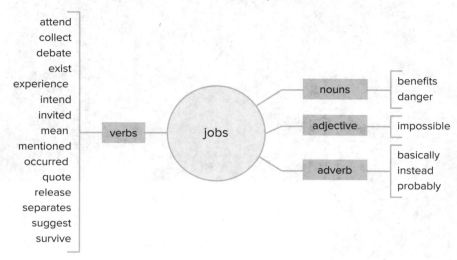

attend
collect
debate
exist
experience
intend
invited
mean
mentioned
occurred
quote
release
separates
suggest
survive

verbs → jobs

nouns — benefits / danger

adjective — impossible

adverb — basically / instead / probably

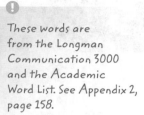

These words are from the Longman Communication 3000 and the Academic Word List. See Appendix 2, page 158.

Listening to Compare

When you listen, it's important to pick out key words that show comparisons. Sometimes the comparisons are direct, when the speaker uses words like *better* or *best*. Sometimes the comparisons can be less obvious, such as when the speaker says one thing is *good* and another is *bad*. Here are three ways of listening to compare.

- Listen for adjectives. Ask yourself if other things are mentioned in the same way or in a different way. For example: miners need *strong* bodies; lawyers need *strong* minds.

- Listen for comparative adjectives that show one of two things is different than the other. These include many *-er* forms of words, such as *bigger* and *smaller*, or comparisons that use *more* plus an adjective, such as *more intelligent*.

- Listen for superlative adjectives that show one thing is different than two or more things. These include many *-est* forms, such as *biggest* and *smallest*. Superlatives sometimes use *most* plus an adjective, such as *most intelligent*.

A. Some adjectives have irregular comparative and superlative forms. They must be memorized. Fill in the missing words in the table. Look up those you don't know.

ADJECTIVES	COMPARATIVE FORM	SUPERLATIVE FORM
1 *good*	better	best
2 bad		worst
3 little	less	
4 much		most
5	farther/further	farthest/furthest

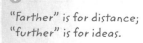

"Farther" is for distance; "further" is for ideas.

© ERPI • Reproduction prohibited

B. Read these sentences and indicate whether each word in bold is an adjective, a comparative, or a superlative.

SENTENCES	ADJECTIVE	COMPARATIVE	SUPERLATIVE
❶ People want **good** jobs.			
❷ Being a logger is the **most dangerous** occupation.			
❸ They may also want **more** challenging jobs.			
❹ Fishers experience a **lower** number of deaths, 81 per 100,000.			
❺ They experience the **highest** number of deaths compared to other occupations.			
❻ Dangerous jobs can be **exciting**.			

C. Listen to an excerpt from Listening 1 about airline pilots. There are two adjectives, two comparatives, and two superlatives. One of each is given below. Write the other ones and then share them with a partner.

ADJECTIVES: _____*different*_____ _____

COMPARATIVES: _____*higher*_____ _____

SUPERLATIVES: _____*most qualified*_____ _____

FOCUS ON CRITICAL THINKING

Recognizing Point of View

When you listen, it's necessary to recognize the speaker's point of view. A point of view is how the speaker feels about a topic. Sometimes there are clues in the title of a talk.

A. Here are the titles of the three listenings in this chapter. Indicate which titles suggest the speaker's point of view. Discuss with a partner.

☐ Some Jobs Aren't Worth It

☐ A Job in Space Debate

☐ Chris Hadfield: Hero Astronaut

It is easier to recognize point of view if you shorten the speaker's ideas. Follow these suggestions.

• Listen carefully to understand the main point, or main points, the speaker makes.

• Ignore examples and explanations.

• Look for adjectives, comparatives, and superlatives that support or oppose the main point or main points.

• Write the speaker's point of view in a short sentence.

© ERPI • Reproduction prohibited

B. Read this excerpt from Listening 1. Use the suggestions given to recognize the speaker's point of view. Highlight adjectives, comparatives, and superlatives, and underline the main points.

> There are many factors involved, and they are different for each profession and for each person. I've already mentioned money, time off, and low barriers to entry. But another factor is a psychological one: dangerous jobs are more exciting and, if you are successful, you are proud of yourself and others admire you.
>
> But I prefer my boring job, teaching university. I may hurt my arms carrying books, but the danger is much smaller.

SPEAKER'S POINT OF VIEW: _____

_____

C. Listening 2 is a debate about space exploration. Listen to an excerpt and use the suggestions above to write each speaker's point of view about the topic.

SPEAKER 1: _____

_____

SPEAKER 2: _____

_____

LISTENING ① Some Jobs Aren't Worth the Costs

Good jobs often have high costs. One cost of becoming a doctor is the money necessary to pay for university. One cost of becoming a musician is years of training. In many cases, money and training may not even help you succeed. Some athletes work for years for a gold medal then miss winning it by a fraction of a second. For many high-paying physical jobs, the costs can be injury or death. What makes a job worth the costs?

VOCABULARY BUILD

In the following exercises, explore key words from Listening 1.

A. Draw an arrow ↓ to indicate where the word in parentheses should be placed in the sentence.

❶ (attend) We were invited, but aren't sure we can .

❷ (danger) There's no if you are a trained scuba diver .

❸ (mentioned) No one that the class was cancelled .

❹ (probably) I'm not sure but I will go to the ice rink .

❺ (survive) To in the woods, you need to stay warm .

B. The words *mean* and *experience* can be used as nouns or verbs.
Fill in the blanks to complete the sentences.

1 I don't know what the questions _____ so I can't answer them.

2 I would like to _____ swimming under a waterfall.

3 His one _____ with monkeys made him scared of them.

4 The _____ income of engineers is much higher.

C. What do the words in bold mean to you? Complete the sentences.

1 What is a **danger** that scares you?

I'm scared of _____

2 What kind of party do you like to **attend**?

I like to attend _____

3 Which event would you like to **experience** this year?

I'd like to experience _____

4 What will you **probably** do this weekend?

I'll probably _____

Before You Listen

A. Read this introduction to Listening 1. Then answer the questions.

> Most people want a good job. They may also want more excitement in their lives. But they don't always want to combine the two. My name is Dr. Kelly Brookes and I research the world of work.

1 Which two things is Dr. Brookes comparing?

_____

2 Write three examples of exciting jobs.

_____

B. Listening 1 compares four jobs: logging, fishing, piloting, and roofing.
Pick two of the jobs and write three things they have in common.

logging    fishing    piloting    roofing

_____

_____

© ERPI • Reproduction prohibited

While You Listen

C. The first time you listen, try to understand the main points about each job. Listen again to complete the descriptions in the comparisons column. Listen a third time to check which jobs are mentioned in terms of the comparisons. Fill in the statistics on number of deaths.

Note: *occupation* is another word for *job.*

COMPARISONS	LOGGING	FISHING	PILOTING	ROOFING
1 danger: *highest number of deaths*				
2 money: _____ _____				
3 seasonal: _____ _____				
4 low barrier to entry: _____ _____				
5 college programs: _____ _____				
6 tests: _____ _____				
7 attend college programs: _____ _____				
8 extensive lessons: *flying hours*				
9 exciting: _____ _____				
10 deaths: *per one hundred thousand*	*111*			

After You Listen

D. Choose the word or phrase that best completes each sentence.

1. The speaker's focus is on _____ jobs.

   a) well-paying

   b) dangerous

   c) boring

2. Seasonal jobs are those that are done _____.

   a) in every season

   b) for most of the year

   c) for part of the year

© ERPI • Reproduction prohibited

3 The number one reason people probably choose jobs is _____.

    a) money   b) excitement   c) fun

4 Learning on the job is common when you _____.

    a) go to a college   b) have passed   c) learn from your
       program   a test   parents

5 The speaker is _____.

    a) a pilot   b) an academic   c) a roofer

6 The speaker compares her own job, suggesting it is _____.

    a) exciting and   b) admired and   c) boring and safe
       dangerous   successful

E. What are the benefits of each job? Form a group of four. Each group member chooses a different job: logging, fishing, piloting, or roofing. Write short notes about the job. Then explain to the other group members why you would want that job.

_____

_____

_____

FOCUS ON GRAMMAR

Prepositions of Time and Place

Prepositions are parts of speech that let you know where something is in time or place. Some prepositions are only for time and some are only for place. But some are for both, including *at, in, on, from, to,* and *for.*

A. Read the explanations for when to use prepositions of *time* and write your own examples. Practise saying your examples with a partner.

PREPOSITIONS OF TIME	EXPLANATIONS	EXAMPLES	YOUR EXAMPLES
at	time on a clock	Class starts **at** 9:00 o'clock.	
in	month, year, season, future time	I graduate **in** four years, **in** 2021.	
on	days of the week, dates	She left **on** Saturday. That was **on** her birthday **on** March 18th.	
for	how long something lasts	She will travel **for** five months.	
from / to	when something starts and ends	The course goes **from** September **to** December.	

© ERPI • Reproduction prohibited

B. Read the explanations for when to use prepositions of *place* and write your own examples. Practise saying your examples with a partner.

PREPOSITIONS OF PLACE	EXPLANATIONS	EXAMPLES	YOUR EXAMPLES
at	address, specific place, area	Let's meet **at** the library.	
in	city, province, state, country, interior space	I study **in** our kitchen.	
on	street	Our apartment is **on** Acorn Street.	
for	how far	We will drive **for** 4,500 kilometres.	
from / to	where something starts and ends	We will drive **from** Calgary **to** Mexico City.	

C. Choose the preposition in parentheses that correctly completes each sentence.

1. (On / In) September 12th, 1962, American President John F. Kennedy explained the reasons for travelling (for / from) the Earth (at / to) the moon.

2. (At / In) 1969, Neil Armstrong became the first man to walk (on / in) the moon.

3. Maybe we'll live (on / to) Mars one day.

4. When Robert Hooke was (in / at) Oxford University (in / at) the 1600s, he made one of the first microscopes.

5. Chris Hadfield was the first Canadian to float freely (on / in) space.

6. Canada was going to have astronauts, so it went (for / from) being a little boy's pipedream (to / at) actually something to do.

My eLab

Visit My eLab to complete Grammar Review exercises for this chapter.

LISTENING ❷   **A Job in Space Debate**

In a discussion, a *devil's advocate* is a person who takes the opposite point of view from the rest of the group. This helps overcome "groupthink," the tendency for people to want to agree about benefits and overlook problems. Many big ideas, like going to Mars, interest people but they may not stop to think about the problems involved in such a trip.

In the following exercises, explore key words from Listening 2.

A. Match each word to its definition.

WORDS		DEFINITIONS
1 benefits (n.)	_____	a) as an alternative
2 collect (v.)	_____	b) advantages or profits
3 instead (adv.)	_____	c) bring together (things)
4 intend (v.)	_____	d) say for others to consider
5 suggest (v.)	_____	e) plan something

B. The suffix -*able* shows that something can be done. For words that end in -*e*, drop the -*e* before adding -*able*. Fill in the blanks with the -*able* form of *collect, debate,* and *quote*.

1 I don't agree and I think the point is _____.

2 His final speech to the students was _____.

3 Buyers suddenly find her art quite _____.

C. What do the words in bold mean to you? Complete the sentences.

1 What do you **intend** to do tonight?

I intend to _____

2 What is one **benefit** of being a student?

One benefit is _____

_____

3 Can you **suggest** a good video to watch?

I suggest _____

4 What's a topic you like to **debate** with friends?

I like to debate _____

Before You Listen

A. Read this introduction to Listening 2. Then answer the questions on the next page.

> **RYAN COOPER:** Hi, I'm Ryan Cooper and welcome to *Devil's Advocate Podcast*. It's where we debate big issues. Today, we have Carla Perez with us. Carla once worked as an engineer at NASA—the National Aeronautics and Space Administration. Welcome, Carla!
>
> **CARLA PEREZ:** Thanks, Ryan. Great to be here.
>
> **COOPER:** So, Carla, let's start the debate. I'd like to suggest that becoming an astronaut is a waste of time and money. I'm hoping you will disagree!

© **ERPI** • Reproduction prohibited

1 What is Ryan Cooper's job?

    a) He is a devil's advocate.

    b) He does podcast debates.

2 What was Carla Perez's old job?

    a) She was an astronaut.

    b) She was an engineer.

3 What topic will they discuss?

    a) They will discuss becoming an astronaut.

    b) They will discuss debates.

4 What will they compare?

    a) They will compare the amount of time and money.

    b) They will compare debates with astronauts.

B. Read the introduction in task A again. Based on what you learned in Focus on Critical Thinking (page 61), indicate which statement represents the two speakers' points of view.

☐ Both speakers are against becoming an astronaut.

☐ Both speakers are for becoming an astronaut.

☐ One speaker is against and one is for becoming an astronaut.

C. Listening 2 compares the benefits of space exploration to the costs. Before you listen, write notes on what you think are the benefits and the costs of space exploration.

BENEFITS	COSTS

While You Listen

D. The first time you listen, try to understand the general idea. While you listen the second time, indicate each person's point of view about each statement in the table. Listen a third time to check your answers. If one of the speakers does not agree or disagree with a statement, leave the space blank.

STATEMENTS	RYAN COOPER'S POINT OF VIEW		CARLA PEREZ'S POINT OF VIEW	
	AGREES	DISAGREES	AGREES	DISAGREES
1 Becoming an astronaut is a waste of time and money.				

© ERPI • Reproduction prohibited

STATEMENTS	RYAN COOPER'S POINT OF VIEW		CARLA PEREZ'S POINT OF VIEW	
	AGREES	DISAGREES	AGREES	DISAGREES
❷ Kennedy gave a great speech.				
❸ A walk on the moon inspired people.				
❹ Practical applications of research come later.				
❺ Most satellites have military uses.				
❻ We should spend more money to help people on Earth.				
❼ Human-made global warming threatens our long-term survival.				

After You Listen

E. Check what you wrote in Before You Listen, task C, about benefits and costs. Were your ideas mentioned in the podcast? Add other points based on what you heard.

F. Choose the word or phrase in parentheses that best completes each sentence, according to the listening.

Neil Armstrong reviews flight plans.

❶ The purpose of the podcast debate is probably to let (Cooper / Perez) share what she knows about the topic of (spending money / space exploration).

❷ The 1962 (speech / podcast) about going to the moon was something to do because it was (easy / hard).

❸ In (1963 / 1969), Neil Armstrong became the first person to (walk on the moon / fly into space).

❹ Armstrong's trip cost (millions / billions) of dollars.

❺ The purpose of the trip was to (collect rocks / do research).

❻ The example of Robert Hooke at Oxford University showed how research leads to (practical applications / better microscopes).

❼ The mention of DARPA was about the invention of (satellites / the Internet).

❽ One long-term benefit of space research is a better understanding of (asteroid crashes / natural global warming).

G. Read the statements in While You Listen again. Which do agree with? Which do you disagree with? Discuss with a partner.

© **ERPI** • Reproduction prohibited

FOCUS ON SPEAKING

Disagreeing Politely

It's important to sometimes disagree, but it's more important to disagree politely. When you discuss a new topic, you need to find ways to express opinions and question ideas. You also need to think critically about the points you hear. Use these expressions when you want to agree or disagree politely.

Pronunciation: Emphasis on different words in a sentence changes the meaning. Practise saying sentences with more emphasis on key words.

My eLab ✎

Visit My eLab to complete a pronunciation exercise.

AGREEING
I agree with you.
That's a good point.
That's true.

PARTLY DISAGREEING
I agree, in part, but …
That's true, but …
That is only partly true.

DISAGREEING
I don't think so.
I'm sorry, but I disagree.
The problem is …

AVOIDING DISAGREEMENT
Let's just move on.
Let's agree to disagree.
Let's drop it.

A. Work with a partner. Choose one of the topics below and take opposite points of view. Practise a conversation with polite disagreement. Each partner should use one item from each of the above four groups of expressions.

TOPIC 1: Becoming an astronaut is a waste of time and money.
TOPIC 2: Instead of going to Mars, we should improve things on Earth.
TOPIC 3: Research needs to have practical applications.

B. Think of a situation in your life where you disagreed with someone. Explain the situation to your partner then role-play a conversation you might have. During the conversation, try to use the above expressions.

WARM-UP ASSIGNMENT
Describe Your Dream Job

You probably have many choices about the jobs you could do. Listening 1 talked about jobs as a logger, a fisher, a pilot, and a roofer. Reasons for doing each job included high salaries, time off, low barriers to entry, and being admired. But there are also costs, such as time, money, and a degree of danger. In this Warm-Up Assignment, you will describe your dream job to a partner.

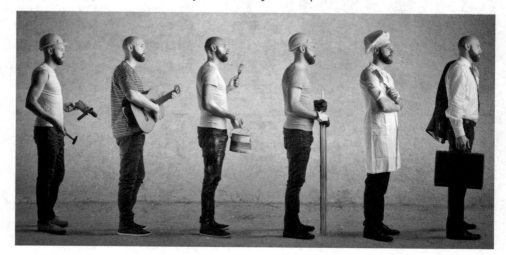

© ERPI • Reproduction prohibited

A. Which qualities do you want in a dream job? Read this list and add two more. Then number the qualities in terms of what is most (1) and least (8) important to you.

_____ being able to be good at the job

_____ having some degree of control or freedom about what you do

_____ receiving fair pay

_____ helping others

_____ working with interesting coworkers

_____ having opportunities to learn

_____ _____

_____ _____

B. Write your dream job and three reasons why the job appeals to you.

MY DREAM JOB: _____

- _____

_____

- _____

_____

- _____

_____

> *Use feedback from your teacher and classmates on this Warm-Up Assignment to improve your speaking.*

C. Write your points as notes. Use what you learned in Focus on Grammar (page 65) to add prepositions of time and place. For example, explain when you would like to do the job (in a few years) and where you would like to do it (at a university).

D. Practise explaining your dream job on your own. Then explain it to a partner.

LISTENING ③   Chris Hadfield, Hero Astronaut

Many astronauts have gone into space and lived aboard the Mir and International Space Stations, but Chris Hadfield has perhaps made the greatest impression. While there in space, the former fighter pilot had more than one million Twitter followers and participated in other social media, often sharing his photos of Earth. He was inspired to become an astronaut after watching the moon landings in 1969. He has since inspired many other people's interest in space.

© ERPI • Reproduction prohibited

In the following exercises, explore key words from Listening 3.

A. Fill in the blanks to complete the sentences.

basically	exist	impossible	release	separates

1. Often a movie _____ comes after the stars promote it on talk shows.

2. Because he knew it was _____, he didn't bother to try.

3. Seasons don't really _____ in Hawaii; it's the same all year long.

4. She shook her head from side to side _____ to say no.

5. The highway _____ one neighbourhood from the other.

B. Match each word to its synonym.

WORDS		SYNONYMS
❶ impossible (adj.)	_____	a) make available to buy
❷ invited (v.)	_____	b) not likely to happen
❸ occurred (v.)	_____	c) pulls apart
❹ release (v.)	_____	d) asked to come
❺ separates (v.)	_____	e) happened

C. What do the words in bold mean to you? Complete the sentences.

1. What can you do to **separate** your studies from your social life?

   I can _____

   _____

3. What invention do you wish **existed**? Why?

   I wish there was _____

   _____

4. Where would you like to be **invited** to visit? Why?

   I'd like to visit _____

   _____

5. What is something that's **impossible** for you to do?

   It's impossible for me to _____

   _____

My eLab ✏

Visit My eLab to complete
Vocabulary Review exercises
for this chapter.

© ERPI • Reproduction prohibited

Canadarm

Before You Listen

A. Read this short summary of Chris Hadfield's life. Then describe him in one sentence.

1959	• Born in Sarnia, Canada, and grew up on a farm.
1978	• Joined the Canadian Armed Forces.
1982	• Earned a Bachelor's degree in mechanical engineering.
1992	• Selected by the Canadian Space Agency as a NASA Mission Specialist.
	• First fully qualified Canadian Space Shuttle crew member.
1995	• First Canadian to operate the Canadarm in space.
	• First Canadian to board a Russian spacecraft and helped add to Space Station Mir.
2001	• First Canadian to perform two spacewalks.
2013	• First Canadian to command the International Space Station.

Chris Hadfield _____

_____

B. Read interviewer George Stroumboulopoulos' introduction to Chris Hadfield. Use what you learned in Focus on Listening (page 60) and underline adjectives to help you recognize Stroumboulopoulos' point of view about Hadfield. Then write a sentence to explain his point of view.

> For 144 glorious days this year, Commander Chris Hadfield orbited the Earth, travelled almost one hundred million kilometres, and refocused the world's attention on the sheer wonder of space travel.

POINT OF VIEW: Stroumboulopoulos _____

_____

C. In Listening 3, Hadfield describes a typical day on the International Space Station. How do you think he would spend each day? Write five things.

• *Get up, get things cleaned up.* _____

• _____

_____

• _____

_____

• _____

_____

• _____

_____

© **ERPI** • Reproduction prohibited

While You Listen

D. The first time you listen, try to understand the general idea. While you listen the second time, write notes to answer the questions. Listen a third time to check your answers and add details.

QUESTIONS	ANSWERS
❶ What did Hadfield release?	*a music video filmed in space*
❷ Who inspired Hadfield when he was young?	*Neil Armstrong*
❸ How many science experiments did Hadfield and his crew perform in space?	
❹ How many Twitter followers did Hadfield have?	
❺ What time did Hadfield talk to mission controls around the world?	
❻ What time did Hadfield go to sleep?	
❼ How long did he repeat his daily routine?	
❽ What was the question Hadfield discussed with his wife?	
❾ What were the two thresholds (limits)?	First, *wake up two mornings in a row and you don't want to go to work.* Second,
❿ What was impossible when Hadfield was nine years old?	
⓫ How old was Hadfield's future wife when he told her he wanted to be an astronaut?	
⓬ When did the chance to go into space become a reality?	
⓭ When did Hadfield's little boy pipedream become a reality?	

After You Listen

E. Check what you wrote in Before You Listen, task C. Add details to Hadfield's typical day on the International Space Station.

© ERPI • Reproduction prohibited

F. Indicate whether these statements are true or false, according to the listening.

STATEMENTS		TRUE	FALSE
1	Hadfield was an astronaut and is also a musician.		
2	Hadfield decided to become an astronaut after he finished university.		
3	Hadfield's Twitter posts from space were popular.		
4	Hadfield's routine in space was quite different every day.		
5	Some days, Hadfield woke up and didn't want to go to work.		
6	Hadfield was an astronaut for twenty-one years.		
7	Hadfield wanted to be an astronaut when he was nine.		
8	The interview is about Hadfield's motivations for being an astronaut.		
9	The main message of the interview is that dreams can come true.		

G. Chris Hadfield inspired many people to become astronauts. In what other topics might he inspire interest? Write two and share with a partner.

_____

_____

Academic
Survival Skill

Working with a Partner

It's valuable to work with a partner. A 2014 study at Stanford University showed that working together has major benefits, especially in terms of motivation. Motivation improves even when partners are not physically together. But when working together, both partners need to understand their roles and the goals. Follow these suggestions for working effectively with a partner.

- Share contact information and calendars. Plan when you will meet to work. Set deadlines for stages of the project, not just a final deadline.
- Give your point of view but be flexible. For example, if you have different ideas about what the assignment is or what you should do for it, find a way to sort through your differences.
- Discuss your skills. Is one of you better at presenting or using a certain computer program? Or do you want to work on a new skill?
- Divide the work and responsibilities. Check to make sure you both feel the amount of work is fair.

© **ERPI** • Reproduction prohibited

A. Read these problems and write notes on what you can say to a partner about each one. Then discuss your solutions with a partner. Use what you learned in Focus on Speaking (page 70) to agree or disagree politely.

PROBLEMS	NOTES ON WHAT I CAN SAY
1 My partner is too busy to get together.	*Let's look at our calendars and find three times we can meet.*
2 I can't do my part until my partner finishes his part—and he's late!	
3 We don't agree on what the assignment is so we can't get anything done.	
4 I'm doing too much of the work and my partner is doing too little.	
5 My partner is sick and can't finish her part on time.	
6 My partner doesn't think the assignment is as important as other things she's doing.	

> **❶** It's best to be polite because sometimes when you disagree, you may be wrong. Always show respect.

> **❶** Remember your goals are to learn and to finish the project, even if you have to do more work than your partner.

B. Work in a group and discuss other problems students have working with partners. What solutions can you find?

FINAL ASSIGNMENT
Compare Two Jobs

Use what you learned in this chapter to explain your dream job to a partner. Then compare your dream job with your partner's dream job.

A. Based on the feedback you received on your Warm-Up Assignment, consider how you can improve your explanation of your dream job.

B. As you and your partner explain your dream jobs, use what you learned in Focus on Listening (page 60) to find things you can compare. For example, talk about how dangerous each job is. Use adjectives, comparatives, and superlatives to make the comparisons. Write notes in the table.

© ERPI • Reproduction prohibited

	MY DREAM JOB	MY PARTNER'S DREAM JOB
ADJECTIVES		
COMPARATIVES		
SUPERLATIVES		

C. Use what you learned in Focus on Speaking (page 70) to politely disagree with your partner about the two jobs. For example, if your partner says that her dream job as a doctor has better pay, you may partly disagree and point out other advantages of your job.

Example: My dream job is to be a doctor. Doctors are better paid than teachers. I partly agree, but teachers don't have the same university costs and are able to start working sooner.

D. After you have explained and compared your dream jobs, reflect on what you could improve about your explanation and discussion skills.

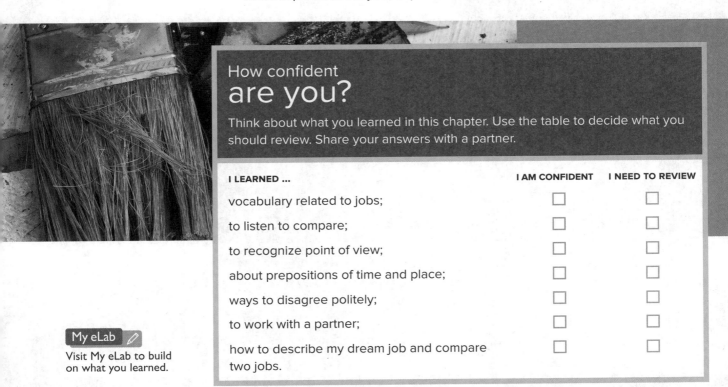

How confident are you?

Think about what you learned in this chapter. Use the table to decide what you should review. Share your answers with a partner.

I LEARNED ...	I AM CONFIDENT	I NEED TO REVIEW
vocabulary related to jobs;	☐	☐
to listen to compare;	☐	☐
to recognize point of view;	☐	☐
about prepositions of time and place;	☐	☐
ways to disagree politely;	☐	☐
to work with a partner;	☐	☐
how to describe my dream job and compare two jobs.	☐	☐

My eLab 🖊

Visit My eLab to build on what you learned.

CHAPTER 5

Where Will You Live?

The basics of life are often described as food, clothing, and shelter. Around the world, all three show great variation as people adapt to local needs and resources. In terms of shelter, the idea used to be "bigger is better." But today, more and more people think that "smaller and smarter is better." Many buildings are increasingly constructed with concern for the environment, using new materials and technologies that make them both efficient and enjoyable. In future, where will you live and work?

In this chapter, ## you will

- learn vocabulary related to shelter and technology;

- listen for opinions;
- understand non-verbal clues;
- review conditionals;
- express an opinion;

- learn how to work in groups;
- present your opinion and discuss it in a group.

GEARING UP

A. Look at the diagram and then answer the questions.

Around the World, How Big is a House in m²?

Average house size by country

Hong Kong 45
United Kingdom 76
Japan 95
France 112
Canada 181

❶ Which country has the largest homes and which has the smallest homes?

_____

_____

❷ Why might homes be bigger in some countries?

_____

_____

❸ Why might homes be smaller in some countries?

_____

_____

❹ In a cold climate, is it better to have a larger home or a smaller one?

_____

_____

B. Discuss the questions and your answers, first with a partner, then in a group.

Below are the key words you will practise in this chapter. Check the words you understand and then underline the words you use.

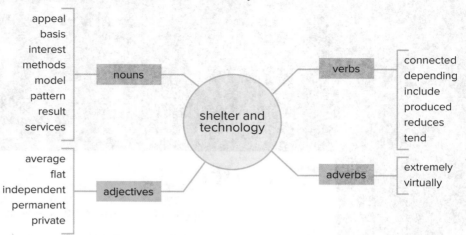

nouns
appeal
basis
interest
methods
model
pattern
result
services

adjectives
average
flat
independent
permanent
private

shelter and technology

verbs
connected
depending
include
produced
reduces
tend

adverbs
extremely
virtually

These words are from the Longman Communication 3000 and the Academic Word List. See Appendix 2, page 158.

FOCUS ON LISTENING

Listening for Opinions

It's common to hear someone speak in a convincing way. Other times, people share an opinion with an uncertain or questioning tone of voice. But it's important to listen to the details and decide whether you are hearing opinions that are just personal or whether they are supported with facts.

Opinions are what people feel about a topic. Often, opinions are preferences. If someone says, "Small houses are better," someone else can say, "Big houses are better." There is no point arguing unless supporting facts are added.

Facts are things that are generally accepted as being true. Often, facts are established through research and experiments. But sometimes they are accepted because they are logical. No one has visited a star, but we understand and accept that stars exist.

When deciding whether you are hearing opinions or facts, listen for key words. Opinions often include adjectives, comparatives, and superlatives and words like *believe*, *should* and *think*. Facts often include words about data, dates, history, numbers, science, and statistics.

A. Listen to four statements. Which of the four speakers give an opinion?

☐ Speaker 1   ☐ Speaker 2   ☐ Speaker 3   ☐ Speaker 4

B. Listen to an excerpt from Listening 1 on the cost of housing over the years. Listen for opinions. Take notes below. Discuss your answer with a partner.

_____

_____

_____

© **ERPI** • Reproduction prohibited

Understanding Non-Verbal Clues

Critical thinking involves more than just understanding what you hear. You also need to understand body language and gestures that add to what people say. For example, sometimes people say "yes," but unconsciously shake their heads "no."

A. Match each photo to a description. Then practise the expressions with a partner.

_____ amused

_____ politely interested

_____ shocked at what you say

_____ surprised

_____ disagreement with what you say

As you speak, you may change your position from open body language (showing interest) to closed body language (rejecting ideas). An example of closed body language is photo 5, above.

B. Read the following gestures and indicate whether they show open or closed body language.

BODY LANGUAGE	OPEN	CLOSED
❶ crossing arms or legs		
❷ leaning away		
❸ leaning forward		

BODY LANGUAGE	OPEN	CLOSED
❹ looking away		
❺ smiling		
❻ standing with arms and legs straight		

C. When listeners show closed body language, you can stop speaking and ask what they think. Or you can use the opposite body language, such as nodding when they are shaking their heads. With a partner, take turns reading these six opinions aloud and practising using open and closed body language. Discuss how the body language affects the message.

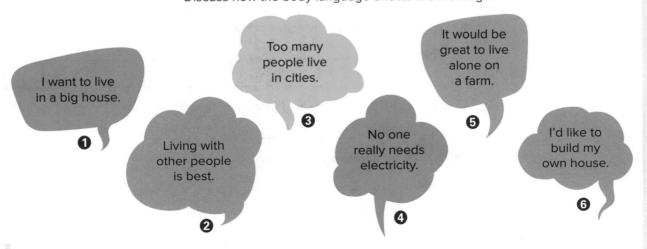

I want to live in a big house. ❶

Living with other people is best. ❷

Too many people live in cities. ❸

No one really needs electricity. ❹

It would be great to live alone on a farm. ❺

I'd like to build my own house. ❻

You might chose a smaller home because it is easier to maintain, cheaper to furnish, or because it has a smaller environmental impact. Some families find smaller homes encourage more interaction, as there are fewer rooms to be alone in. What is the smallest space you could live in?

VOCABULARY BUILD

In the following exercises, explore key words from Listening 1.

A. Match each word to its definition.

WORDS		DEFINITIONS
❶ appeal (n.)	_____	a) typical
❷ average (adj.)	_____	b) happen in a certain way
❸ basis (n.)	_____	c) attraction
❹ tend (v.)	_____	d) way something is done

B. Choose the word in parentheses that is the antonym of the word in bold. Look up words you don't know in a dictionary.

❶ It caught the world's **interest**.   (boredom / attention)

❷ Please **include** the cost of moving my piano.   (ignore / involve)

❸ He needed a **permanent** home for his cat.   (long-term / short-term)

❹ The **appeal** of the house was its six bedrooms.   (upside / downside)

C. What do the words in bold mean to you? Complete the sentences.

❶ What type of news story usually catches your **interest**?

I'm usually interested in _____

❷ What's something you like to **include** in your lunch?

I like to include _____

❸ What's the **appeal** of living on campus?

The appeal is _____

_____

❹ Which quality is the **basis** of a good friendship?

One quality is _____

❺ What's the **average** time you spend on homework?

I spend _____

❻ What type of **permanent** work would you like?

I would like _____

© **ERPI** • Reproduction prohibited

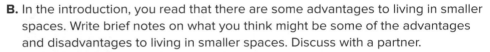

Before You Listen

A. Read this excerpt from Listening 1 about capsule hotels. Underline the phrases that indicate the writer's opinion. Then write a sentence to explain his point of view about capsule hotel rooms.

> In 1979, a strange capsule hotel opened in Tokyo. It caught the world's interest because the hotel's "rooms" were comically small boxes: 2 by 1 by 1.25 metres. No one would want to stay for a long-term visit. At that time, the typical guest was a business person who missed the last train home and needed a cheap place to stay.

_____

_____

B. In the introduction, you read that there are some advantages to living in smaller spaces. Write brief notes on what you think might be some of the advantages and disadvantages to living in smaller spaces. Discuss with a partner.

ADVANTAGES	DISADVANTAGES
lower cost to buy	*lacks room for possessions*

While You Listen

C. The first time you listen, try to understand the general idea. Listen again to the reasons supporting each point or opinion. Based on the facts, indicate whether you agree or disagree. Listen a third time to check your answers.

POINTS AND OPINIONS	AGREE	DISAGREE
1 The appeal of living in smaller spaces has increased.		
2 The cost of a house has gone up over the years.		
3 People now have less money to spend.		
4 In downtown areas, prices for the smallest apartments are foolishly high.		
5 Small homes are great for people who travel for summer or winter vacations.		
6 If housing costs rise, more people will look for alternatives.		
7 Several generations can live happily together.		
8 Cooperative housing with shared spaces is an attractive option.		
9 It's likely your future will be in a smaller home.		

After You Listen

D. Review what you wrote in Before You Listen, task B, on the advantages and disadvantages to living in smaller spaces. Check whether your ideas were covered in Listening 1.

E. Discuss your answers to While You Listen, task C, with a partner. Do you have the same answers? Why or why not?

F. Indicate whether these statements are true or false, according to the listening.

STATEMENTS	TRUE	FALSE
1 The listening asks what people will do if they can't find a place to live on a permanent basis.		
2 One reason for living in smaller spaces is to have a simpler lifestyle.		
3 Micro houses are about 45 metres square in size.		
4 Inspiration comes from Japan where people have larger families.		
5 A century ago, it was common for several generations to live together.		
6 Cooperative spaces include places where people share bedrooms and bathrooms.		

G. Choose the fact from Listening 1 that best supports each opinion.

1 Capsule hotels are popular because they are _____.
   a) mostly located near train stations
   b) less expensive than traditional hotels

2 People now have less money to spend because _____.
   a) of the cost of other things like cars and college
   b) they are not saving as much money

3 Micro houses are great for vacations because _____.
   a) people can put them on trailers
   b) they can be built of plastic

4 People question how much they need because they _____.
   a) realize extra bathrooms are little used
   b) have large families and need more beds

5 Generations should live together because _____.
   a) there is always someone to cook
   b) people can take care of each other

6 Your future will likely include a smaller home because _____.
   a) the cost of large homes are about the same
   b) the cost of homes continues to rise

© ERPI • Reproduction prohibited

Conditionals

Grammar helps you express different ideas. Sometimes you want to talk about what **usually** happens **if** you do something. Other times, you want to talk about what **will** happen **if** you do something. In both cases, you use a form of the conditional tense. Consider the table.

TYPE	IF-CLAUSE	RESULT CLAUSE	EXAMPLES
ZERO CONDITIONAL IF = WHENEVER	simple present	simple present	**If** someone **comes** to the door, the dog **barks**.
FIRST CONDITIONAL REAL OR POSSIBLE	simple present	future with *will*	**If** you **come** to the door today, the dog **will** bark.

A. Choose the correct form of the verb in parentheses to complete these sentences: simple present or future tense. Then write 0 for the zero conditional or 1 for the first conditional.

1. But if you're on the Internet, I'd say you (are / will be) still on the grid. _____

2. If housing costs continue to rise, more people (look / will look) for alternatives. _____

3. If I want to go off grid, where (do / will) I start? _____

4. If you're serious, you (start / will start) with a small home that's easy to heat. _____

5. What (do / will) they choose if they cannot afford a house next year? _____

B. Complete these questions and then practise asking and answering them with a partner.

1. ZERO CONDITIONAL: What do you do if _____ happens?

2. FIRST CONDITIONAL: If you _____, what will happen?

My eLab 🖉

Visit My eLab to complete Grammar Review exercises for this chapter.

LISTENING ❷   It's Time to Rethink Our Homes

There have always been people who left the comfort of cities to live in remote places. Now technologies are making it easier for people to live anywhere, such as using solar panels to generate local power. The term *grid* refers to all the public services that used to be necessary to make a house practical, such as electricity. Could you live off the grid?

© **ERPI** • Reproduction prohibited

In the following exercises, explore key words from Listening 2.

A. Choose the best definition for the word in bold.

1. Two old **methods** have to do with building walls.
   a) choices made by mistake in the past
   b) certain procedures for doing things

2. In many parts of the world, some **services** still aren't available.
   a) necessary payments made every month
   b) assistance provided by an official organization

3. Living off the grid means not **depending** on public utilities.
   a) needing support from
   b) feeling sorry for

4. Many off-gridders are closely **connected** to other people.
   a) spread apart over a large distance
   b) brought together or into contact

B. Choose the word in parentheses that is the synonym of the word in bold. Look up words you don't know in a dictionary.

1. The architect is **independent** and works on her own.   (free / needy)
2. His phone number is **private**, only available to friends.   (public / reserved)
3. The two islands were **connected** by a long bridge.   (linked / separated)
4. Working on a team **reduces** work for everyone.   (increases / lessens)

C. What do the words in bold mean to you? Complete the sentences.

1. What makes you feel **independent**?

   I feel independent _____

   _____

2. What **method** do you use to take notes?

   I take notes by _____

3. How are you **connected** to friends and family?

   I'm connected by _____

4. What helps **reduce** your stress?

   I reduce stress by _____

5. Which public **services** are important to you?

   The services I use are _____

   _____

6. What is something you would always keep **private**?

   I would keep _____

© ERPI • Reproduction prohibited

Before You Listen

A. Listening 2 talks about new ways of building homes. For example, rammed earth walls are made by compressing layers of earth. Another method to make walls is by covering hay with clay (straw bale walls). Both have advantages for keeping homes warm and cool. List some of the advantages and disadvantages of building your own home. Then discuss with a partner.

rammed earth wall

straw bale walls

ADVANTAGES	DISADVANTAGES
you can find cheap materials	

B. A focus of Listening 2 is living off the grid. This means not depending on public services that are so important to many city homes. Besides electricity, write three other common services that cities offer.

_____

_____

C. Which services would you miss most if you lived off the grid? Choose from your answers to task B. Explain your reasons to a partner.

While You Listen

D. Listen the first time to understand the general idea. Then read the questions and the answers in the table. While you listen the second time, indicate which answers Sloan gives to Trent's questions. Listen a third time to confirm your answers.

TRENT'S QUESTIONS	SLOAN'S ANSWERS
❶ What's your definition of living off the grid?	☐ not depending on public utilities, especially the supply of electricity ☐ Wi-Fi ☑ sewers ☐ in many parts of the world, services aren't available
❷ Okay, so what did I get wrong?	☐ not all off-gridders live in the country; some live in cities ☐ off-gridders are mostly farmers ☐ many work online

© ERPI • Reproduction prohibited

TRENT'S QUESTIONS	SLOAN'S ANSWERS
❸ The way I see it, if you're on the Internet, I'd say you're still on the grid.	☐ there are degrees of going off grid ☐ some live in log cabins ☐ some live in tents ☐ that's too extreme
❹ What else do you think? I guess you're more modern.	☐ use modern architecture and technology ☐ live in a 60 square metre prefab home ☐ prefab homes assembled in a factory and put up wherever ☐ reduces waste and keeps costs down ☐ uses a special toilet ☐ use a wood-burning stove, solar panels, a windmill
❺ OK. If I want to go off grid, where do I start?	☐ ask yourself why ☐ private ☐ independent ☐ fun ☐ have a change
❻ But I could live off the grid in the city, you said?	☐ a small home easy to heat ☐ save money
❼ Can you give me other examples?	☐ bales of straw ☐ rammed earth ☐ keep you cool in summer and warm in winter
❽ You also mentioned technology.	☐ use software to figure out where to put windows ☐ use software to put in doors
❾ In my opinion, living off the grid sounds like a lot of work.	☐ millions of people do it ☐ if more people start doing it, costs will come down

After You Listen

E. Review your answers in Before You Listen, task C, and in While You Listen. Which services were mentioned and which were not? Discuss with a partner.

_____

_____

_____

F. Choose the word or phrase that best completes each sentence.

❶ One fact about living off the grid is _____.

a) no one needs electricity

b) services often aren't available

c) everyone has sewers

© ERPI • Reproduction prohibited

2 Off-gridders live _____.

   a) in the country

   b) in the city

   c) everywhere

3 The phrase "degrees of going off the grid" suggests _____.

   a) most are extreme

   b) some are extreme

   c) none are extreme

4 Reducing waste likely appeals to off-gridders _____.

   a) concerned about the environment

   b) who work in business fields

   c) who have large families

5 Asking yourself why you want to live off the grid is important because _____.

   a) you might live with others

   b) it's usually short-term

   c) it's a big decision

6 If more people choose to live off the grid, it will _____.

   a) lead to fewer cities everywhere

   b) lower the costs of doing so for everyone

   c) lead to more farming in cities

G. You now know many facts about living off the grid. Would you want to try it? Why or why not? Use facts from Listening 2 to support your opinions and discuss them with a partner.

FOCUS ON SPEAKING

Expressing an Opinion

In Focus on Listening, you learned about opinions. You are often asked for your opinion. For example, a friend might ask if you like something, such as yogurt. This is a personal opinion without a right or wrong answer. In other situations, you might be asked to support your opinion with facts. This kind of opinion is common in classroom discussions, as in task G above.

There are several ways to introduce your opinion. Use these phrases to signal to your listeners that you are expressing an opinion, and that opinions may or may not be supported by facts.

- I think …
- If you ask me …

- In my opinion …
- The way I see it …

Similarly, there are several ways to ask others about their opinions.

- Do you agree?
- What are your ideas?

- What do you think?
- What's your opinion on … ?

The word "because" often connects opinions with facts.

© ERPI • Reproduction prohibited

A. Work in a group. Look at the photos and take turns expressing your opinions about each one. For example, would you want to live there? Why or why not? Discuss the advantages or disadvantages.

Japanese castle

floating home

old house

tents

When you hear people share opinions, ask follow-up questions, particularly if they have not supported their opinions with facts to form valid opinions. Use these phrases.

- Do you have any facts to back up your opinion?
- Do you have reasons for feeling that way?
- Is there any support for your opinion?
- What makes you think that?

> A "valid opinion" is an opinion supported with facts.

B. Discuss the photos in task A again. Ask follow-up questions about the opinions of your group members.

WARM-UP ASSIGNMENT
Present Your Opinion

It is easy to have an opinion; it's more difficult to support that opinion with facts. In this Warm-Up Assignment, you will present your opinion on where you would like to live and support it with facts.

A. In Listening 1 and 2, you heard about different places people live or stay, such as capsule hotels. Choose one of the following as a place you'd like to live.

capsule hotel

traditional house trailer house apartment rammed earth house multi-generation house micro house off grid house straw bale house

My choice is _____

© ERPI • Reproduction prohibited

B. Consider one aspect of the place you chose and write your opinion about it. Your opinion might have to do with cost, size, comfort, or whether it is suitable for families, whether or not you would like to live there, or whether it makes environmental sense to live there.

Example: I'd like to live in a straw bale house because I could build it myself.

_____

_____

C. Find three facts to support your opinion. Use what you learned in Focus on Grammar (page 85) to include an example of the conditional.

- _____

  _____

- _____

  _____

- _____

  _____

Use feedback from your teacher and classmates on this Warm-Up Assignment to improve your speaking.

D. Present your opinion and supporting facts to a partner. Use phrases that you learned in Focus on Speaking (page 89). Emphasize your points with non-verbal clues you learned in Focus on Critical Thinking (page 81). Ask for feedback on what you could improve.

LISTENING ❸ Buildings That Breathe: Doris Sung's Living Architecture

Doris Sung is an architect who is interested in new building materials. Among these are flexible metal panels that change shape with heat. This allows them to let in more light or air. This kind of solution to an old problem is not just practical, it's beautiful. Would you rather live in an older traditional house, or something new that looked like a piece of art?

VOCABULARY BUILD

In the following exercises, explore key words from Listening 3.

A. Draw an arrow ↓ to indicate where the word in parentheses should be placed in each sentence.

❶ (extremely) He was upset when he lost his work .

❷ (flat) Although the office had some round walls , others were .

❸ (virtually) We couldn't see him in person , but his image appeared .

❹ (produced) They asked for the work in a month and we it on time .

❺ (pattern) The was made up of large and small circles .

© ERPI • Reproduction prohibited

B. The words *model* and *result* can be used as nouns or verbs. Fill in the blanks with the correct word to complete the sentences.

1 Using weak materials will _____ in the building falling down.

2 The small _____ shows what the apartment will look like.

3 We can use software to _____ the shape of each window.

4 The final _____ of the vote made her the winner.

C. What do the words in bold mean to you? Complete the sentences.

1 What work have you **produced** this week?

I produced _____

2 What was your best **result** on an assignment this year?

My best result was _____

3 What's something you find **extremely** exciting?

I'm excited by _____

4 When is it useful to make a **model** of something?

I'd make a model _____

5 What's a **pattern** you like on clothes?

I like _____

My eLab

Visit My eLab to complete Vocabulary Review exercises for this chapter.

Before You Listen

A. In this excerpt from Listening 3, Doris Sung talks about architecture being static (unchanging). Underline the phrases that show Sung's opinions.

> I think, growing up, I thought of architecture as being extremely static. Buildings did not conform to the human body, nor to human nature. So my question, when I finally got to architecture school and out, to this very day, is why can't architecture accommodate the human? Maybe it's a lot better if we make it respond, so that looking at a building, and considering it more like a skin.

B. This listening deals with a technical subject. Technical subjects often use jargon—professional language. Some jargon is taken from other languages. Here are three examples from the listening. Read the sentences and guess the meaning of the word in bold.

1 We were really dedicated to trying to use **Grasshopper** from beginning to end in this project. So not only was it useful in making the form, but it was very useful all the way down to determining the files and the fabrication files of the tiles.

a) small jumping insect

b) software program

c) material for making tiles

2 So if you can imagine on a south-facing or a west-facing glass wall system, these bimetal walls can be either inserted within the glass system, within what we call a double-skin facade, or even on the outside as a ***brise soleil***.

a) sun shade   b) bright sun   c) type of cheese

© ERPI • Reproduction prohibited

3 They can start to shade ... which is a big deal because we have a lot of heat gain—especially in Los Angeles, where I am—to the sun from the outside. And it would lower costs for air conditioning, and in effect and indirectly, also reduce the amount of **heat island** effect.

a) place close to the equator surrounded by water

b) place in a home where the stove is located

c) somewhere much hotter than surrounding places

C. One focus of the listening is how flexible metal panels can react to heat and change shape. Read the words and their definitions and highlight the ones that are related to heat.

1 400 degrees: high temperature

2 bimetals: two metals put together

3 heat gun: construction tool that shoots hot air

4 laminated: layered together

5 pivot: change from one position to another

6 shading: protection from the sun

7 solar: related to the sun

8 penetration: how far something can enter

9 sundial: tool for telling time using the sun

10 thermal: to do with heat

11 tiles: flat shapes made of clay or other material

12 ventilation: flow of air

While You Listen

D. Listen the first time to understand the general idea. Then read the points and partial comments in the table. While you listen the second time, fill in the blanks to complete the comments. Listen a third time to check your answers.

POINTS	COMMENTS
1 **QUESTION:** Why can't architecture accommodate the human?	• better if we make architecture ___*respond*___ • building is more like a ___*skin*___
2 **CHALLENGE:** to compete in the world of building technology	• research, design, use thermal ___*bimetals*___ in architecture
3 **EXPLANATION:** metals expand when heated	• when two alloys are heated, one will expand _____ • result: the metal _____
4 **EXAMPLE:** metal on a lamp	• bulb gave off enough heat so the hood of the lamp _____
5 **OPINION:** Why can't we use this as a surface material to architecture ...	• to control the air for ventilation • or for _____

© **ERPI** • Reproduction prohibited

POINTS	COMMENTS
6 **EXAMPLE:** when you start to heat it up with our heat gun	• all the pieces start _____ • the material pivots at about _____ degrees • continues curling until _____ degrees
7 **EXPLANATION:** Bloom was trying to make a project that would actually be outside and react to the sun.	• shape is like a sundial • circular or radial shape facing _____ at different times of day and can _____ • because of differences the surface _____ in different ways
8 **TOOL:** Use Grasshopper from beginning to end in this project.	• useful in making the form and the files for the tiles • _____ tiles of bimetal; all are _____ • _____ different frame pieces
9 **EXPLANATION:** pattern making and variation built into the software	• model connected with _solar analysis_ tool • red areas have _____ exposure to the sun • without these _____ could not produce Bloom
10 **QUESTION:** imagine on a south-facing or a west-facing glass wall system ...	• bimetal walls can be either inserted _____ or _____ (_brise soleil_) the glass system
11 **EXPLANATION:** They can start to shade—automatically and with zero energy.	• a lot of _____ in Los Angeles • _____ costs for air conditioning • _____ the amount of heat island effect

After You Listen

E. Connect the phrases to summarize Listening 3.

SUMMARY		
1 Doris Sung is ...	_____	a) it works automatically and uses zero energy.
2 Her interest in bimetals ...	_____	b) demonstrate the technology.
3 The complex shapes mean they are ...	_____	c) an architect who works with new technologies.
4 The bimetals allow for ...	_____	d) difficult to create by hand.
5 The Bloom project was probably just to ...	_____	e) shading and ventilation.
6 An attraction of the bimetal technology is that ...	_____	f) is related to how they change shape with heat.

© ERPI • Reproduction prohibited

F. Complete these sentences to explain Sung's goal in working with bimetal technology. Discuss your answers with a partner.

① Doris Sung works with metals that _____

_____

② She uses strips of these metals to make skins _____

_____

G. Sung's work is experimental. Why do you think she does not do more practical architecture, such as designing traditional homes and offices?

_____

_____

_____

Academic
Survival Skill

Working in a Group

Working in a group is common both in the classroom and in the workplace. Group work often focuses on a shared project. Sometimes that project is divided into parts that each group member can complete separately. But when you meet and discuss or work on a project, it's important to use listening and speaking strategies to make sure the project is completed efficiently (on time) and effectively (in the best way possible).

An important part of working in a group is choosing or assigning roles. This usually means having a group leader who is responsible for organizing meetings and making sure they flow smoothly. Other roles, like taking notes, checking the time, and organizing a schedule, will be necessary depending on the purpose of the group.

A. Imagine meeting three other students for the start of a project. Number these steps in the order in which you would follow them.

_____ Introduce yourselves and exchange contact information.

_____ Choose or assign the role each group member will have.

_____ Set a time and place for the next meeting.

_____ Explain the project.

_____ Identify deadlines—times when smaller parts of each member's work needs to be completed.

_____ Discuss how the work can be divided.

© **ERPI** • Reproduction prohibited

B. Read this dialogue from a group meeting and indicate the step for each line. Use the numbering from task A.

GROUP DISCUSSION	STEPS
① **RAY:** Hi, I'm Ray and this is Kim. What's your name?	_____
② **JEN:** I'm Jennifer. Good to meet you both.	_____
③ **KIM:** Yes. So, let's talk about our project. It focuses on sharing our opinions about architecture. Does everyone agree?	_____
④ **JEN:** Yes, but we also have to discuss our opinions.	_____
⑤ **KIM:** Right. How do you think we should divide up the work?	_____
⑥ **RAY:** Well, we each need to write out our opinion.	_____
⑦ **JEN:** Maybe we could do that by Wednesday.	_____
⑧ **KIM:** That sounds good. Then we can meet again, maybe at four o'clock in the library.	_____
⑨ **RAY:** Sure. Then we share our opinions and write follow-up questions by Thursday. Do either of you have anything to add? Any other questions? Then I think we're done.	_____

In the dialog, there are four follow-up questions. These questions are used to find out more information. They also help improve group relationships by showing respect for the ideas and questions of each group member.

- Does everyone agree?
- How do you think we should divide up the work?
- Do either of you have anything to add?
- Any other questions?

C. Form a group of three. Take the roles of Ray, Jen, and Kim and act out the dialog as it is written. Then act it out again but add your own answers to the follow-up questions. Use non-verbal clues you learned in Focus on Critical Thinking (page 81).

! Pronunciation: Words ending with "s" can have different pronunciations: "s," "z," "IZ." Listen for the differences in these words: "yes," "does," "focuses."

My eLab ✎
Visit My eLab to complete a pronunciation exercise.

FINAL ASSIGNMENT
Discuss Your Opinion

Use what you learned in this chapter to present and discuss your opinion from the Warm-Up Assignment in a group.

A. Form a group of three. Follow the first steps of the Academic Survival Skill: discuss the assignment and choose a group leader. Apart from being one of the three speakers, the group leader will introduce and close the discussion.

Example: Today, let's share opinions on places to live. Each of us shares an opinion and, after everyone has spoken, we'll ask questions.

B. When it is your turn to speak, present your opinion and the supporting facts that you prepared for the Warm-Up Assignment (page 90) to the group. Use phrases that you learned in Focus on Speaking (page 89). Emphasize your points with non-verbal clues (see Focus on Critical Thinking, page 81).

© ERPI • Reproduction prohibited

C. While you listen to the other speakers, take notes in the table below. Listen for key words that indicate opinions and facts (see Focus on Listening, page 80). Think of questions to ask.

SPEAKER 1: CHOICE AND OPINION	
SPEAKER 2: CHOICE AND OPINION	
SPEAKER 3: CHOICE AND OPINION	
QUESTION FOR SPEAKER 1	
QUESTION FOR SPEAKER 2	
QUESTION FOR SPEAKER 3	

D. When all group members have presented, ask your follow-up questions and answer questions that group members ask you. Use phrases you learned in Focus on Speaking (page 89).

E. Reflect on the discussion. What could you improve?

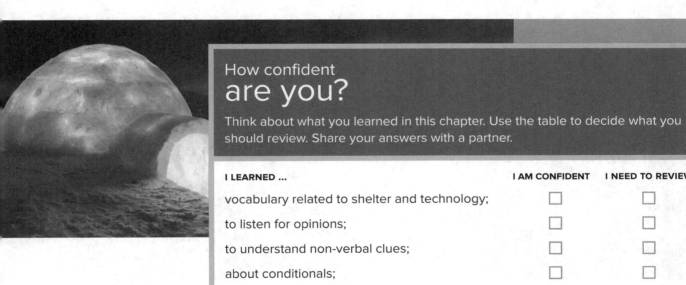

How confident are you?

Think about what you learned in this chapter. Use the table to decide what you should review. Share your answers with a partner.

I LEARNED ...	I AM CONFIDENT	I NEED TO REVIEW
vocabulary related to shelter and technology;	☐	☐
to listen for opinions;	☐	☐
to understand non-verbal clues;	☐	☐
about conditionals;	☐	☐
to express an opinion;	☐	☐
how to work in groups;	☐	☐
how to present an opinion and discuss it in a group.	☐	☐

My eLab ✎
Visit My eLab to build on what you learned.

CHAPTER 6
Earth, Your Home

A metaphor for Earth is that it is a spaceship, with limited resources to make its endless journey. A century ago, few people worried about running out of resources like oil. Nor did they worry about polluting the land, air, or water. Even when people did worry, their concerns were mostly about local issues. Now we see the world as an interconnected set of problems and opportunities—including cultural ones—and realize we are all responsible for them. What kind of world do you want to live in?

In this chapter,
you will

- learn vocabulary related to views of the world;

- listen to infer the meaning of words;

- connect new ideas to what you know;

- ask questions using modals;

- prepare a set instructions;

- ask questions in a lecture;

- present and discuss instructions in a group.

GEARING UP

A. Look at the infographic about energy and the environment. Then answer the questions.

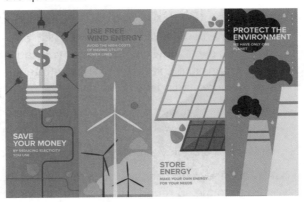

① What is one way you could reduce your use of electricity?

_____

_____

② The infographic suggests wind energy is free, but it still costs money to build windmills. Why do some people think wind is a good power option?

_____

_____

③ You can store energy with a large home battery. What would be an advantage of having a powerful home battery?

_____

_____

④ What is a current threat to the environment?

_____

_____

B. Discuss the questions and your answers, first with a partner, then in a group.

Below are the key words you will practise in this chapter. Check the words you understand and then underline the words you use.

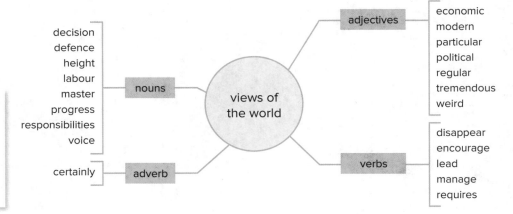

These words are from the Longman Communication 3000 and the Academic Word List. See Appendix 2, page 158.

views of the world

nouns
- decision
- defence
- height
- labour
- master
- progress
- responsibilities
- voice

adverb
- certainly

adjectives
- economic
- modern
- particular
- political
- regular
- tremendous
- weird

verbs
- disappear
- encourage
- lead
- manage
- requires

FOCUS ON LISTENING

Listening to Infer the Meaning of Words

There are more than a million words in English and about 8,500 are added each year. You can't know all of them but you can infer—or guess—the meaning of many through simple strategies. These strategies include listening for the context—the surrounding words.

You already listen for words in context when you sort out the differences between homonyms—words that sound the same but are spelled differently.

Example: I **read** a book yesterday. I have a **red** book.

In both sentences, *read* and *red* are pronounced the same way, but you know as you listen to the surrounding words that they mean different things. Here are some ways to infer the meaning of words.

- Listen for paraphrases of a word—when the speaker uses another word or phrase to clarify the word. Often, paraphrases use the phrase *which means* or the word *or.*

- Listen for words made up of roots or words that you know. For example, you may guess that the root *aud-* in *audio* has to do with hearing. That helps you understand the meaning of words like *audience, audition,* and *auditory.*

- Listen for contrasts in a phrase, sentence, or paragraph that suggest the new word is the opposite of another better-known word.

- Listen for the type of word and decide how important it is: nouns and verbs are more important to understanding a sentence; adjectives and adverbs are less important. In any case, knowing the part of speech helps you guess its meaning.

A. Listen to four excerpts from Listening 3. Based on what you can infer from the context, write short definitions for each word.

1. deities (n.): _____

2. ritual (adj.): _____

3. notions (n.): _____

4. locomotion (v.): _____

© **ERPI** • Reproduction prohibited

B. Share your definitions with a partner. Then check a dictionary to see if you were correct.

C. Listen to the four excerpts again and match each word to the way you can infer its meaning.

WORDS		WAYS TO INFER MEANING
❶ deities	_____	a) an adjective
❷ ritual	_____	b) root words
❸ notions	_____	c) contrasting word
❹ locomotion	_____	d) paraphrase

FOCUS ON CRITICAL THINKING

Connecting New Ideas to What You Know

When you listen, it's natural for you to connect new ideas to those you already know. This is called *activating prior knowledge* and it helps make new information more meaningful. Follow these tips to make connections to new information.

- Ask yourself if you have a personal connection to the ideas you hear. For example, if the country China is mentioned, perhaps you, or someone you know, visited China, or maybe you have a friend from China.
- Ask yourself how an idea connects with what you already know. For example, do you know certain facts about China, such as its place on a map of the world?
- Make connections between familiar and unfamiliar ideas you hear. For example, you might hear China mentioned along with a city called Lijiang and assume Lijiang is in China.

A. Read this excerpt from Listening 1. Underline the words and phrases that have a personal connection for you. Highlight the ideas that connect to what you know.

Let's begin in ancient China. Like other early civilizations in Egypt and what is now modern-day Iraq, water was essential to growing crops. But it was not enough for farmers to find some water in a river or a lake and carry it to their plants. The use of water had to be organized with a high degree of cooperation.

B. Indicate which ideas are connected.

IDEAS	COUNTRIES	GROWING	WATER
China			
crops			
Egypt			
farmers			
Iraq			
lakes			
plants			
rivers			

© ERPI • Reproduction prohibited

C. A Know-Wonder-Learn (KWL) chart is one way to connect new ideas to what you know and what you don't know. It's a good tool to use when you listen to lectures and, after, when you study. Read this paragraph and then fill in the table. After, discuss your answers with a partner.

> Most countries expand and contract over time like heartbeats. Sometimes they disappear. In 1920, the British Empire had colonies in Africa, Australia, Canada, India, and elsewhere. It covered almost 24 percent of the world's land. By comparison, the Roman Empire at its height only covered 3.36 percent of the world. But things change. Today 77 countries are larger than Great Britain.

WHAT I KNOW	WHAT I WONDER ABOUT	WHAT I LEARNED
	Why do countries expand, contract, and disappear?	

LISTENING ❶   What about Water?

What makes people live together in large numbers? The earliest people lived in groups for safety and to share resources, like farmland and water. Today, people live in cities to take advantage of all the services and opportunities for work and pleasure. As people's lives become more digital, working and being social online, do you think they will live closer or farther apart?

VOCABULARY BUILD

In the following exercises, explore key words from Listening 1.

A. Fill in the blanks with the correct words to complete the paragraph.

decision	manage	modern	regular	requires

In the _____ world, once in a while you need to make a

_____ that people won't like. A difficult choice often _____

that you convince people of why your point of view is correct. Sometimes a

_____ argument isn't enough. If you want to _____ a team

effectively, you need to show through an example how your ideas could work.

B. The words *lead* and *labour* can be used as nouns or verbs. Fill in the blanks to complete the sentences.

❶ The _____ we put into organizing this project will help get it done on time.

© ERPI • Reproduction prohibited

2 He has the _____ in the race; everyone else is far behind him.

3 These days, fewer people _____ at the same job for forty years.

4 She was asked to _____ the team to the top of the mountain.

C. What do the words in bold mean to you? Complete the sentences.

1 What kind of **modern** music do you like?

I like _____

2 Which subject **requires** the most work?

The subject is _____

3 What is a difficult **decision** for you to make?

A difficult decision is _____

4 Which group or team would you like to **lead**?

I'd like to lead _____

Before You Listen

A. Listening 1 is about how water has shaped society. Look at this photo of a harbour near Marseilles, France. Why is water so important to society? How does water help people live and work together happily? Make notes then discuss with a partner.

_____

_____

B. In Focus on Critical Thinking (page 101), you organized ideas using a KWL chart. Read these four issues from Listening 1 and write notes on what you wonder about. After you listen, fill in details about what you learned about each point.

WHAT I KNOW	WHAT I WONDER ABOUT	WHAT I LEARNED
1 Managing water was the root of many civilizations because organizing things like systems for watering farms makes people work together in the long-term.	*How do farmers figure out how to share water?*	
2 Civilization happens when we help each other because cooperation benefits everyone.		
3 As societies get bigger, taxes allow governments to hire people for special jobs.		
4 Things that happen once may lead to something that makes them happen again, in a cycle.		

© **ERPI** • Reproduction prohibited

C. In Listening 1, Dr. Eaves is asked this question: "What happens as global warming continues to affect river systems and farms?" What do you think will happen? Choose the best answer.

☐ People are likely to move away from areas where there is no longer as much water.

☐ People will fight over limited water supplies and, in some cases, countries will go to war.

☐ With the help of scientists, people will find new ways to farm with less water.

While You Listen

D. The first time you listen, try to understand the general idea. Listen a second time for the sentences with key words in bold. Use what you learned in Focus on Listening (page 100) to infer the meanings of the words in bold. Listen a third time to check your inferences and add details.

SENTENCES WITH KEY WORDS	INFERRED MEANINGS
❶ Rice **paddies** are flooded when the seedlings are planted. They have to be watered on a regular basis.	*field where rice is planted*
❷ Other farmers, farther away, have to get the water to flow through a **ditch** across the first farmers' lands.	
❸ Some **scholars** suggest that managing water was the root of many civilizations.	
❹ Could **flooding** also lead to cooperation?	
❺ For the **establishment** of dikes along rivers, it was important for people to work together.	
❻ Trees and other plants send roots down that help hold the **soil** together.	
❼ Also, it takes a lot of materials and the **labour** of hundreds of people to build a dike.	
❽ And with taxes, and people in charge, and workers doing **diverse** jobs, groups start to form governments.	
❾ But what happens today when things don't go right and start to **deteriorate**.	
❿ And we've seen the same thing **transpire** many times in the past.	

© **ERPI** • Reproduction prohibited

After You Listen

E. Go back to Before You Listen, task B, and add notes in the last column: What I Learned. Then review your answer to task C. Discuss with a partner to see if you had the same or different points.

F. Choose the phrase that best completes each sentence.

  1 Besides China, Dr. Eaves mentions examples in _____.

    a) Canada and Mexico

    b) Japan and Korea

    c) Egypt and Iraq

  2 The main problem in the lecture comes from _____.

    a) too much water

    b) too little water

    c) many kinds of water

  3 From the use of rice as an example, it seems likely that rice _____.

    a) needs more water than many other crops

    b) can be grown without the use of water

    c) needs the same amount of water as other crops

  4 Farmers who lived next to a river had _____.

    a) many disadvantages in terms of access to water

    b) less room in which to grow rice in paddies

    c) advantages over farmers who were farther away

  5 Laws and taxes seem to be natural outcomes of _____.

    a) farmers who choose not to grow rice in paddies

    b) people organizing themselves to do different jobs

    c) farmers wanting to be in charge of other people

  6 Global warming is listed as a threat because _____.

    a) taxes would have to be higher for cooling costs

    b) too many people would start farming rice

    c) affected farms could produce less food

G. Water management was an old reason for people working together and helping each other. What is a modern reason that people form communities and help each other?

_____

_____

© ERPI • Reproduction prohibited

FOCUS ON GRAMMAR

Ask Questions Using Modals

In Listening 1, Louise Erazo interrupted Dr. Eaves with Twitter questions from the class. Many of these questions used modals, like *can, could, should,* and *have to.* Modals are used to help ask about ability, permission, possibility, advice, and obligation.

A modal is an auxiliary verb used with a main verb in its base form. *Can, could,* and *should* can be used as the first words of a question. The modal *have to* is used with *do* or the question words *who, what, when, where, why,* and *how.*

MODALS	MEANINGS	EXAMPLES
can	permission for choices	**Can** I present next?
	ability to do something	**Can** you tell me what "conquer" means?
could	possibility of something	**Could** there be another reason?
should	asking for advice	**Should** I read this chapter?
have to (has to)	obligation, without a choice	Do you **have to** study? Who **has to** help you?

A. Choose the modal in parentheses that correctly completes each question.

1. (Have to / Can) you imagine why?

2. (Should / Could) flooding also lead to cooperation?

3. What did early peoples (have to / should) do about floods?

4. (Could / Should) we believe that things will carry on the way they were?

5. What (can / should) you see happening?

6. What (have to / has to) be completed before Monday?

7. (Could / Can) there be more than one answer to that question?

B. Fill in the blanks with the correct modals to complete this excerpt from Listening 2. Then practise saying the questions with a partner.

can	could	have to	should

_____ you explain why an ecological view of the world is more important than a political or an economic one? _____ you give an example of how an ecological view _____ benefit a political or commercial situation? _____ economies always continue to grow? Do you _____ accept the world as it is or _____ you work together to change it?

Visit My eLab to complete Grammar Review exercises for this chapter.

© ERPI • Reproduction prohibited

LISTENING ❷ Three Ways to Look at the World

In 1972, the crew of the Apollo 17 spacecraft took a picture of what they called the "Blue Marble." It was the first full picture of Earth from space. It looked different than the globe that sits in most classrooms. When you are young, the world seems a large and mysterious place. Over time as you travel and learn, you see it differently. What is your view of the world now?

VOCABULARY BUILD

In the following exercises, explore key words from Listening 2.

A. Match each word to its definition.

WORDS		DEFINITIONS
❶ defence (n.)	_____	a) top of something
❷ disappear (v.)	_____	b) expression of an opinion
❸ height (n.)	_____	c) no longer visible
❹ voice (n.)	_____	d) resisting attack

B. Draw an arrow ↓ to indicate where the word in parentheses should be placed in the sentence.

❶ (particular) He has a approach to arranging his stamp collection .

❷ (political) The duties of a prime minister and a president are similar .

❸ (economic) The country's policies include spending more on education .

❹ (voice) He was the of the government .

❺ (height) The company was losing money at the of the recession .

C. What do the words in bold mean to you? Complete the sentences.

❶ What is a **particular** food you like?

I like _____

❷ What is a problem you wish would **disappear**?

I wish _____

❸ What is your **height**?

My height is _____

❹ What local **political** problem interests you?

One problem is _____

© ERPI • Reproduction prohibited

CHAPTER 6 Earth, Your Home **107**

Before You Listen

A. Listening 2 introduces three views of the world. Indicate how each of the actions could affect the world in an ecological, an economic, or a political way. Some actions have more than one effect.

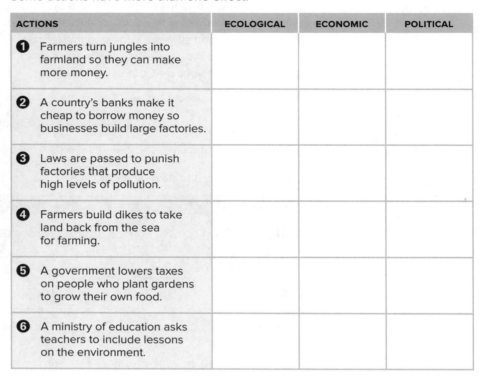

ACTIONS		ECOLOGICAL	ECONOMIC	POLITICAL
❶	Farmers turn jungles into farmland so they can make more money.			
❷	A country's banks make it cheap to borrow money so businesses build large factories.			
❸	Laws are passed to punish factories that produce high levels of pollution.			
❹	Farmers build dikes to take land back from the sea for farming.			
❺	A government lowers taxes on people who plant gardens to grow their own food.			
❻	A ministry of education asks teachers to include lessons on the environment.			

B. In Focus on Critical Thinking (page 102), you used a KWL chart to connect ideas. You can use a mind map in the same way. Fill in the blanks with what you know about the topics (K), what you wonder about (W), and, after you listen, what you learned (L). Add extra bubbles for new ideas. Here are some words and phrases to help you think.

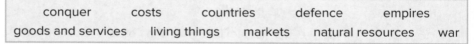

conquer	costs	countries	defence	empires
goods and services	living things	markets	natural resources	war

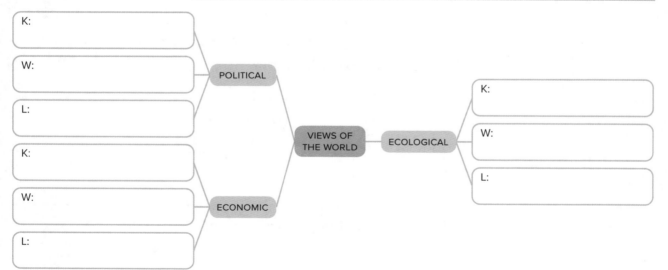

© ERPI • Reproduction prohibited

While You Listen

C. The first time you listen, try to understand the general idea. While you listen the second time, take notes on the points Dr. Burns talks about. Write whether they are political, economic, or ecological views. Try to infer the meaning of the words given. Listen a third time to check your notes and add details.

SECTIONS	NOTES AND INFERENCES
1 As I said, today's topic is three ways to look at the world ... Let's start with political.	*People's views based on their expertise.* *expertise = what they are experts about*
2 Most countries expand and contract over time like heartbeats ... Today seventy-seven countries are larger than Great Britain.	political: _____ colonies = _____
3 How do countries change in size ... The major reason for such wars relates to our second point of view ...	_____ : _____ swell = _____
4 An economic view sees the world in terms of goods and services and ways to buy and sell them ... After a time, locals would rebel and start a new war.	_____ : _____ routes = _____
5 Political and the economic views are closely tied. The third view, ecological, is different ... The big question is whether those costs are worth the benefits.	ecological: _____ habitat = _____
6 These are important issues ... Here are some questions for you.	_____ : _____ duties = _____

After You Listen

D. Consider your answers in Before You Listen, task B. Add ideas that you have learned.

E. Indicate whether these statements are true or false, according to the listening.

STATEMENTS	TRUE	FALSE
1 People's perceptions of the world are based on their areas of expertise.		
2 The British Empire is an example of how countries get bigger and smaller over time.		
3 An economic view of the world is based on the borders around countries.		
4 One step in developing markets is to build roads and railways.		
5 The ecological view of the world is the same as the political and economic views.		
6 The idea of "having a voice" is about keeping your concerns to yourself and not making them public.		

© ERPI • Reproduction prohibited

F. Near the end of Listening 2 are four questions. Answer the questions and then discuss your answers with a partner.

1 Can you explain why an ecological view of the world is more important than a political or an economic one?

_____

_____

2 Could you give an example of how an ecological view can benefit a political or commercial situation?

_____

_____

3 Should economies always continue to grow?

_____

_____

4 Do you have to accept the world as it is or can you work together to change it?

_____

_____

FOCUS ON SPEAKING

Giving Instructions

Instructions are steps for how to do something. It's common to hear instructions before a test. Instructions tell you what you have to do, the order in which you have to do it, as well as things you should not do, or have to be careful about. Follow these suggestions when you are giving instructions.

- Define unusual vocabulary. Look up words you don't know in a dictionary.
- Use transition words, like ordinal numbers, to show where one step ends and another begins: _first, second, third_.
- Use transition words to indicate you have reached the end of your steps: _finally, lastly, in the end_.
- Add explanations where necessary.
- Mention any dangers using words like _remember, always, never_.
  Example: **Never** leave a fire unattended.

A. In Listening 1, Dr. Eaves talked about how to construct a dike. Number these sentences (including on page 111) in the correct order.

_____ A dike is a long wall to prevent flooding.

_____ But you have to be careful; dikes need to be maintained. If there is one weak spot, they can fail.

_____ Finally, once the dike is finished, you often plant things on it.

_____ First, you decide how long the wall should be, and how high.

© ERPI • Reproduction prohibited

⓵

Pronunciation: The letters "th" can be pronounced in two ways, ð like in "the" or θ like in "third." Listen for the differences.

My eLab 🖉

Visit My eLab to complete a pronunciation exercise.

_____ Third, you gather enough people to complete the building job before the next flood.

_____ Trees and other plants send roots down that help hold the soil together.

_____ Second, you choose the materials to build the dike, usually the base is stone and higher portions are dirt and mud.

B. Read the sentences in task A again. Underline new ideas, explanations, and dangers. Highlight transition words.

C. Look at these visual instructions for making tea. Work with a partner and practise explaining the steps. Introduce the topic, use transition words, and conclude with what you should always or should never do. Use the words *teabag, teapot, cup, temperature, time, sugar*, and *lemon*. *Milk* is not included but you could mention that as well.

100 °C

WARM-UP ASSIGNMENT
Prepare a Set of Instructions

When you see people lost or looking at a map, you may offer to help by giving instructions that they can follow to reach their destination. In this Warm-Up Assignment, you will prepare a set of instructions on a topic of your choice and present it to a partner.

A. Choose a topic. Listenings 1 and 2 talked about ecological issues. Choose something related to the environment that you could give a set of instructions on. Here are some sample topics, but you can choose one of your own.

☐ how to collect rainwater   ☐ how to compost

☐ how to grow a plant   ☐ how to recognize one kind of insect

☐ how to recycle   ☐ how to save energy at home

☐ Other _____

B. Write your instructions following the steps you learned in Focus on Speaking.

- Look up unfamiliar terms in a dictionary and include short definitions.
- Use transition words to show where one step ends and another begins. Use other transition words to show the end of your steps.
- Include anything that a listener might have to pay careful attention to.

Use feedback from your teacher and classmates on this Warm-Up Assignment to improve your speaking.

C. Check your instructions.

☐ Did you define unusual vocabulary?

☐ Did you use transition words to show where one step ends and another begins?

☐ Did you mention any dangers?

D. Read your instructions aloud and then present them to your partner.

LISTENING ③ The World View of Wade Davis

Wade Davis is a Canadian explorer and ethno-botanist, who studies the relationship between cultures and the plants they use. His work has taken him to wilderness settings around the world. In one of his many books, and photo collections, he tells people to, "Risk discomfort and solitude for understanding." Davis has spent his life trying to understand the ways people live and the effects on the world around them.

VOCABULARY BUILD

In the following exercises, explore key words from Listening 3.

A. Fill in the blanks with the correct words to complete the sentences.

certainly	encourage	responsibilities	tremendous	weird

❶ She didn't like the new fruit because she thought it was _____.

❷ To get fit, they _____ us to walk to school or work each day.

❸ The fireworks went off with a _____ bang.

❹ His _____ included taking care of all the plants in the garden.

❺ Explain your problem to the teacher; she will _____ help you.

B. The words *progress* and *master* can be used as nouns or verbs. Fill in the blanks to complete the sentences.

❶ If you want to _____ in English, it helps to practise as much as possible.

❷ They started by greeting the _____ of the martial arts class.

❸ I tried to _____ Spanish by working at a Peruvian restaurant.

❹ The broken paddle limited her canoe's _____ along the river.

C. What do the words in bold mean to you? Complete the sentences.

❶ What is one of your main **responsibilities**?

One is _____

© **ERPI** • Reproduction prohibited

2 Which TV show do you think is **weird**?

I think _____

3 What could you do to **progress** faster in your studies?

I could _____

4 When are you **encouraged** to do your best?

I'm encouraged _____

My eLab

Visit My eLab to complete Vocabulary Review exercises for this chapter.

Before You Listen

A. Read this excerpt from Listening 3. Based on the context, what can you infer about the meaning of the three words in bold? Check a dictionary to confirm your answers.

> I try to encourage students to realize that there's no such thing as creativity. I mean, creativity doesn't exist in the **abstract**; it's a consequence of action. And do what's necessary to be done, and then ask whether it was possible, or **permissible**, for that matter. And in that way, you end up really being the master of your own life. And I certainly—at my age of fifty-nine—I can look back, and I see the bitterness comes to those who look back on a long life of decisions **imposed** upon them.

1 abstract (adj.): _____

2 permissible (adj.): _____

3 imposed (v.): _____

B. Davis talks about the contrast between Australian Aboriginal and British cultures when they first came into contact in 1770. At that time, the Western world was largely unaware of Australia. What do you think they thought about each other?

A modern-day Australian Aboriginal in traditional dress

What Aboriginals thought about Westerners:

_____
_____
_____
_____

Captain James Cook (1728–1779)

What Westerners thought about Aboriginals:

_____
_____
_____
_____

© **ERPI** • Reproduction prohibited

C. Write a sentence that describes the culture of your country. Compare your description with those of other students.

_____

_____

While You Listen

D. The first time you listen, try to understand the ideas. While you listen a second time, take notes on what you learned. Listen a third time to add details.

WADE DAVIS' IDEAS	WHAT I LEARNED
1 a mountain was a pile of rock ready to be mined	
2 interaction between human beings and the natural landscape	_there are consequences for the ecological footprint_
3 Aboriginal people of Australia	
4 the purpose of the Aboriginal universe	
5 put a man on the moon	_is related to climate change because of the industry necessary to make such achievements happen_
6 our way of thinking of the Earth as sort of being inanimate came from somewhere	_Descartes_
7 ideas of myth, and magic, and mysticism	
8 tribal societies	
9 Everest and walking to a point where you can't breathe for lack of oxygen	_illustrates the fragile nature of our environment_
10 exploration	
11 a career is not something	
12 creativity	
13 master of your own life	_a long life of decisions imposed upon them_
14 the word "job" comes from	
15 the word "work" comes from	

After You Listen

E. Review what you wrote in Before You Listen, task B. Compare your answers to the ones that Davis gave in the interview. Do you have similar or different ideas? Why? Discuss with a partner.

© ERPI • Reproduction prohibited

F. Choose the word or phrase in parentheses that best completes each sentence. Use your notes from While You Listen to help you.

1 The example of mountains is used to suggest that Westerners (do / don't) see mountains as living things.

2 Wade uses the example of Australian Aboriginal and British attitudes toward progress to show how they have (similar / different) views of the world.

3 The point about the British shooting Aboriginals was to explain how the British saw Aboriginals as not having the same Western (human / animal) qualities.

4 Aboriginal attempts to keep everything the way it was is an example of (respect / ignorance) for nature.

5 The point about the lack of oxygen on Everest was to illustrate how (thick / thin) the atmosphere is.

6 The idea that you are "the architect of your life" means that you are responsible for building it into what (you want / everyone wants) it to be.

7 Having decisions made for you will make you bitter because you have (no free choice / too many choices).

8 Wade's message at his daughter's graduation was to encourage students to (work for / inspire) themselves.

G. Below is the final sentence of the interview. What does it mean to you? What do you think is your creative destiny? Discuss with a partner.

> "So I've always said to everybody, never have a job, but work harder than anybody you've ever met and out of that will come your creative destiny."

Academic
Survival Skill

Asking Questions in a Lecture

It's easy to sit quietly and *not* ask questions in a lecture. Even if they don't understand what a teacher is saying, students sometimes prefer not to interrupt. They may worry the question sounds silly. Don't be one of those students. Instead, look for opportunities to learn more by engaging your teacher with requests for clarifications, explanations, and examples. Follow these suggestions for asking questions in a lecture.

• Understand if questions are welcome. Often the teacher will begin by saying, "You're welcome to ask questions as I talk" or "Please save your questions until the end." Teachers tend to welcome questions during a lecture with smaller groups; they tend to save them to the end with larger groups.

• Write out your question and make it as short and easy to understand as possible.

• Listen! Be sure to listen to other students' questions. If you don't, you can end up asking the same question again.

• Pay close attention to the answer, keeping eye contact with the teacher. Nod to show you understand. If you don't understand, you may choose to ask a follow-up question or ask your question later, after the lecture.

© **ERPI** • Reproduction prohibited

A. You can ask questions in a lecture in different ways. Read these questions from Listening 1 and match each one to the reason for asking it.

QUESTIONS		REASONS FOR ASKING
❶ Sorry, why taxes?	_____	a) to ask for an explanation with *who, what, when, where, why,* or *how*
❷ How would they make a dike?	_____	b) to identify a topic and then include a question
❸ Dr. Eaves, you talk about rivers. Could flooding also lead to cooperation?	_____	c) to make a question clearer by offering an example of what you are asking about
❹ Excuse me, Dr. Eaves. But what happens today when things fall apart? For example, what happens as global warming continues to affect river systems and farms?	_____	d) to briefly clarify one word or idea

B. Use the following reasons to write short and clear questions about the topics given. Make sure your questions are easy to understand.

❶ to ask for an explanation with *who, what, when, where, why,* or *how*: Aboriginal universe

_____

_____

❷ to identify a topic and then include a question: primitive technology

_____

_____

❸ to make a question clearer by offering an example: choices / example, going to university

_____

_____

❹ to briefly clarify one word or idea: ethos

_____

C. Practise the questions in tasks A and B with a partner. Then try using the same structures to ask new questions.

FINAL ASSIGNMENT
Discuss Instructions

Use what you learned in this chapter to present and discuss your set of instructions from the Warm-Up Assignment in a group.

A. Based on feedback you received on your Warm-Up Assignment, consider how you can improve your set of instructions.

© ERPI • Reproduction prohibited

B. Review the suggestions on how to organize and give instructions that you learned in Focus on Speaking (page 110).

C. Plan how you will present your instructions. Keep these steps in mind and make notes.

STEPS	SAMPLE SENTENCES
Give the topic of your instructions. Explain why you are interested in the topic or why it is important.	Today, I would like to talk about … I'm interested in … because … This is important because …
Introduce the instructions. Remember to use transition words between steps.	Here are instructions for you to follow.
While you give your instructions, pause after important steps to check that your listeners understand. If not, explain in other words.	Do you understand? Is that clear to you?
End with a final transition word and any other important information.	Finally, … Remember, you should/shouldn't …
Ask for questions.	Now, do you have any questions?

D. Use your notes to practise presenting your instructions. Then present and discuss your instructions in a group.

E. As you listen to other students, use what you learned in Focus on Critical Thinking (page 101) to connect to what you already know about their topics. Use what you learned in Focus on Grammar (page 106) and in Academic Survival Skill (page 115) to ask questions. Try to use modals.

F. After, review your presentation and think about what you could improve on.

How confident are you?

Think about what you learned in this chapter. Use the table to decide what you should review. Share your answers with a partner.

I LEARNED …	I AM CONFIDENT	I NEED TO REVIEW
vocabulary related to views of the world;	☐	☐
to listen to infer the meaning of words;	☐	☐
to connect new ideas to what I know;	☐	☐
to ask questions using modals;	☐	☐
how to prepare instructions;	☐	☐
how to ask questions in a lecture;	☐	☐
how to present and discuss instructions in a group.	☐	☐

My eLab 🖉

Visit My eLab to build on what you learned.

CHAPTER 7
Be a Perfect Human

You've heard about people with exceptional abilities—geniuses that think of new and complex ideas and professional athletes that show extreme strength and endurance. Researchers try to understand how some people seem to have surprising talents, such as artist Stephen Wiltshire. He is called "the human camera." He can glance at a city briefly and then draw it in detail. In what ways would you like to be better?

In this chapter,
you will

- learn vocabulary related to physical and mental abilities;
- listen for details about charts;

- predict to listen effectively;
- review the present perfect tense;
- learn how to structure a presentation;

- learn to talk with graphic organizers;
- talk about a new habit and discuss it in a group.

GEARING UP

A. Look at the diagram about weight and cardio (heart rate) training and then answer the questions.

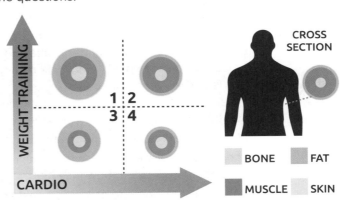

1. Which workout is the best for lowering fat?

   _____

2. Which workout looks least effective? Why?

   _____

   _____

3. How would you describe workout number 4?

   _____

   _____

4. Which workout appeals to you? Why?

   _____

   _____

B. Discuss the questions and your answers, first with a partner, then in a group.

Below are the key words you will practise in this chapter. Check the words you understand and then underline the words you use.

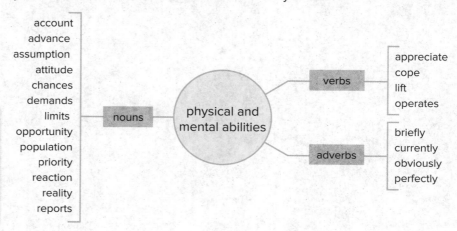

nouns
- account
- advance
- assumption
- attitude
- chances
- demands
- limits
- opportunity
- population
- priority
- reaction
- reality
- reports

physical and mental abilities

verbs
- appreciate
- cope
- lift
- operates

adverbs
- briefly
- currently
- obviously
- perfectly

> These words are from the Longman Communication 3000 and the Academic Word List. See Appendix 2, page 158.

FOCUS ON LISTENING

Listening for Details about Charts

It's common to attend lectures where a speaker uses visual support. This support sometimes includes physical objects but, more often, a computer presentation with graphic organizers, like charts. In smaller presentations, the speaker may use paper charts or draw on a whiteboard. However, speakers often use a chart as a starting point for giving more information. Use this information to help you follow what a speaker is talking about.

- Look at the chart. Focus on the type of information the chart usually shows.

- Look for a title and a legend (explaining the meaning of the chart's colours or patterns). Consider how they help you understand the chart.

- As you listen, note the order the speaker uses to organize ideas. For example, left to right, top to bottom, or clockwise—going around in a circle like the hands of a clock. Also listen to see if sections and key words are mentioned.

- Listen for key words that show the speaker is adding information that's not covered in the chart. For example, words and phrases like *also*, *another thing*, and *something else*.

> Speakers often offer additional information in the form of examples.

A. Look again at this chart from Gearing Up. Draw arrows to label the parts.

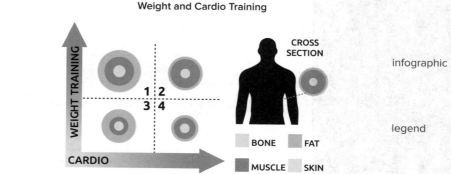

Weight and Cardio Training

title

chart

WEIGHT TRAINING

CARDIO

1 | 2
3 | 4

CROSS SECTION

BONE | FAT
MUSCLE | SKIN

infographic

legend

© **ERPI** • Reproduction prohibited

Listen for changes in tone of voice when a speaker says something new about a chart.

B. Now listen to a woman talking about the chart in task A. Number the phrases in order. Which tell you to look at part of the chart and which tell you that the information is not on the chart?

POINTS	ORDER	IN THE CHART	NOT IN THE CHART
Another thing is that ...			
It doesn't say this, but ...			
Something else is that ...			
The legend shows ...			
You can see this chart shows ...			

FOCUS ON CRITICAL THINKING

Pronunciation: Some words have silent letters, like the "k" in "know." Other words with silent letters include "listen" (t) and "wrong" (w).

Visit My eLab to complete a pronunciation exercise.

Predicting to Listen Effectively

Before you listen to a talk, it's important to gather information and predict what will be said. This helps you listen more effectively. Follow these suggestions.

fortune sticks

- Identify the topic and think about how it relates to something you already know, but stay open to new ideas.
- Consider the title and introduction, and any photos, charts, and illustrations. Think how each of them helps you predict what the talk will be about.
- If the talk has questions, review the questions beforehand. Think how the questions can help you predict what will be important in the talk.
- Check your predictions as you continue to listen to see if you were correct. If you weren't, reflect on what you got wrong.

A. Here are the titles of the three listenings in this chapter. Look up any words you don't know and then try to predict what each listening will be about. Discuss your predictions with a partner.

Listening 1, "Learning from Savants" is about _____

_____

_____

Listening 2, "Human Physical Limits" is about _____

_____

_____

Listening 3, "How to Have a Good Day" is about _____

_____

_____

© **ERPI** • Reproduction prohibited

B. Read this introduction from Listening 3. Think of three things you can predict about what the listening will cover. Discuss with a partner.

> Everyone has good days and bad days. But do some people have more bad days than others? Or is it just to do with your way of looking at the world? What would it take for you to turn bad days into good days?

• _____

_____

• _____

_____

• _____

_____

LISTENING ❶ Learning from Savants

Imagine you could read a book and remember every word. Kim Peek is someone who has this amazing skill. He's done this with 7,600 books. How would that ability help you? This is one of the many abilities a savant can have. *Savant* means *knowledgeable person*, but many savants often lack other abilities we take for granted. Scientists research savants' brains to understand ways we could all be better.

VOCABULARY BUILD

In the following exercises, explore key words from Listening 1.

A. Read each word in bold in context and match it to its definition.

WORDS		DEFINITIONS
❶ His calculation took into **account** the missing days.	_____	a) works
❷ Many people like him are unable to **cope** with the most basic things.	_____	b) consideration
❸ She's found ways to **appreciate** how animals see the world.	_____	c) without any mistakes
❹ They're questions about how the brain **operates**.	_____	d) recognize something's importance
❺ He was playing Tchaikovsky's Piano Concerto No. 1—**perfectly**.	_____	e) manage

© **ERPI** • Reproduction prohibited

B. The words *briefly, obviously,* and *perfectly* are adverbs. Fill in the blanks to complete the sentences.

1. They planned the job _____ and nothing went wrong.

2. I only saw her _____ for a minute or two on the bus.

3. They were _____ early, two hours before the party started.

4. _____ look at these paintings and tell me if you like one of them.

5. The teacher _____ forgot to give them the test but no one complained.

6. I feel _____ well and won't have a problem going to class.

C. What do the words in bold mean to you? Complete the sentences.

1. What's the biggest machine you can **operate**?

   I can _____

2. When do you find it difficult to **cope**?

   One time is _____

3. What is something you can do **perfectly**?

   I can _____

4. What's a quality you **appreciate** in others?

   I appreciate _____

5. If you could **briefly** be someone else, who would you be?

   I'd be _____

Before You Listen

A. Look at this pie chart on the ways people think. Work with a partner to define each part. Then write an example of how you use each one.

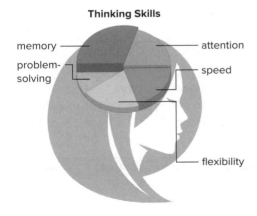

Thinking Skills

memory — attention
problem-solving — speed
— flexibility

THINKING SKILLS	DEFINITIONS	EXAMPLES
attention	*focusing on details*	*listening to one conversation when many people are speaking*
speed		
flexibility		
problem-solving		
memory		

© **ERPI** • Reproduction prohibited

B. Read this excerpt from Listening 1 and answer the questions that follow. Then discuss with a partner.

> Let me start by telling you about Leslie Lemke. He was born early, with severe medical problems. As a baby, he was blind and was unable to speak. It took years for him to learn to stand. He didn't walk until he was fifteen years old. He started to learn to play simple songs on different musical instruments. But when Lemke was fourteen, his parents woke in the middle of the night to the sound of him playing a piece of classical music. They were not even sure how he got from his bed to the piano. He was playing Tchaikovsky's Piano Concerto No. 1—perfectly. He only heard it once on TV, earlier that evening. Since then, Lemke has memorized thousands of songs and has performed internationally. How was this possible?

1 Who is Leslie Lemke?

_____

2 What problems did he have as a baby?

_____

3 When did he start to walk?

_____

4 Where has he performed piano?

_____

5 Why was it unusual for him to play Tchaikovsky's Piano Concerto No. 1 perfectly?

_____

C. Based on what you know from this chapter so far and the title "Learning from Savants," use what you learned in Focus on Critical Thinking (page 121) to predict what the rest of the listening might be about. After you listen, check your answer.

I predict _____

_____

While You Listen

D. Listening 1 talks about seven people with special abilities. While you listen, write each person's special ability. Listen again to check which thinking skills are important to their abilities. Listen a third time and complete the sentences in Notes about the Chart on the next page.

NAMES	SPECIAL ABILITIES	ATTENTION	SPEED	FLEXIBILITY	PROBLEM-SOLVING	MEMORY
Leslie Lemke	*playing piano*	✓	✓			✓
Thomas Fuller						
Kim Peek						
Stephen Wiltshire						
Flo and Kay Lyman						
Temple Grandin						

© **ERPI** • Reproduction prohibited

NOTES ABOUT THE CHART

1. Attention means being able to focus on details by _____.

2. Speed is thinking more _____.

3. Flexibility means thinking about different things _____.

4. Problem solving is about making _____.

5. Memory is about recalling information _____.

After You Listen

E. Choose the word or phrase that best completes each sentence, according to the listening.

1. Leslie Lemke's ability to play the piano was _____.
   a) part of his training
   b) completely unexpected
   c) thanks to good teachers

2. The mention of leap years in Thomas Fuller's answer shows _____.
   a) he didn't understand math
   b) he sometimes made mistakes
   c) his attention to detail

3. Kim Peek's memorization of all the words he has read _____.
   a) does not mean he understands them
   b) shows he is the world's greatest genius
   c) means he can also define each one

4. Stephen Wiltshire's ability to draw things in great detail is _____.
   a) based on exceptional memory
   b) a skill that anyone can learn
   c) useless for artists and designers

5. Flo and Kay Lyman's abilities affect _____.
   a) mostly their hearing
   b) all their senses
   c) how they eat

6. Temple Grandin's special understanding of animals would be important _____.
   a) to be like them   b) to eat them   c) for their care

7. An area of thinking that most of the savants seem to lack is _____.
   a) attention   b) flexibility   c) memorization

8. Being a savant probably means you _____.
   a) fit in well with others
   b) don't fit in well with others
   c) don't want to fit in well with others

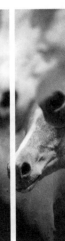

! Every fourth year is a leap year, with one more day in February.

© ERPI • Reproduction prohibited

F. Based on what you now know about savants, answer these questions. Then discuss in a group.

① Which thinking skill would you most like to improve? Why?

_____

_____

② If you had to give up one thinking skill to be a savant, which one would you choose? Why?

_____

_____

FOCUS ON GRAMMAR

Present Perfect Tense

You use the present perfect tense for two reasons. The first is for actions that started in the past and continue in the present.

Example: She **has studied** savants for years.

This means she studied savants in the past and continues to study them now.

The second is for actions that occurred at a time in the past that is not clear.

Example: These individuals **have needed** help.

This means that they needed help in the past but *when* isn't clear.

Form the present perfect tense with the simple present tense of *have* and the past participle of the main verb.

A. Fill in the blanks with the present perfect tense. Use *have* (plural) or *has* (singular) and the past participle of the verb in parentheses.

① Cora (work) _____ with several Olympic competitors.

② The twin sisters remember everything they (see) _____ ever _____.

③ Imagine something similar (happen) _____ to a loved one.

④ These individuals (need) _____ help with simple activities.

⑤ I started to wonder if we (reach) _____ our human limits.

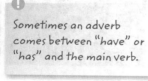

Sometimes an adverb comes between "have" or "has" and the main verb.

Form present perfect questions by changing the word order. Put *have* or *has* at the beginning of the question.

B. Underline phrases in this paragraph that use the present perfect tense.

Many coaches have experimented with mental imagery as a way of improving player performance. Imagine four basketball players. Adele has spent all her practices shooting baskets. Brenda has completed the same hours sitting on the court imagining shooting baskets. Corinne has done half practising and half imagining. And finally, Dara has done nothing—no shooting baskets and no thinking about doing so. The question is, who has benefitted the most after all this training—or lack of training?

© **ERPI** • Reproduction prohibited

C. Write three questions about the paragraph in task B. Use the correct form of the present perfect tense. Then practise asking and answering your questions with a partner.

❶ _____

_____

❷ _____

_____

Visit My eLab to complete Grammar Review exercises for this chapter.

❸ _____

_____

LISTENING ❷ **Human Physical Limits**

You might go to the gym or do other exercise to make yourself stronger or more flexible. Everyone travels an arc from the helplessness of a baby to the reduced abilities of extreme old age. Somewhere along that arc there is a point when you are your most physically fit. But how fit can you be? What limits are there to your physical abilities?

VOCABULARY BUILD

In the following exercises, explore key words from Listening 2.

A. Choose the word or phrase that has the closest meaning to the word in bold.

❶ After all, we **currently** have better tracks.

a) in the past   b) then   c) now

❷ Do you think these limits lower the **chances** of new sporting records?

a) possibilities   b) losses   c) wins

❸ She was able to **lift** a side of the 1,400-kilogram car to free him.

a) lower   b) keep steady   c) raise

❹ It's something found in top-level runners but not in the general **population**.

a) group of athletes   b) group of people   c) audience

B. The words _advance_, _limits_, and _reports_ can be used as nouns or verbs. Fill in the blanks to complete the sentences. Then indicate whether the word is used as a noun or a verb.

SENTENCES	NOUN	VERB
❶ The worker wanted an _____ on his pay.		
❷ The deadline _____ how much we can get done.		

© ERPI • Reproduction prohibited

SENTENCES		NOUN	VERB
❸ I have three _____ about the new diet that say it doesn't work.			
❹ The class is ready to _____ to the next level.			
❺ After a group discussion, one student _____ to the class.			
❻ Are there _____ to the number of students in each group?			

C. What do the words in bold mean to you? Complete the sentences.

❶ What idea **currently** interests you?

I'm interested in _____

❷ What are your **chances** of getting a perfect mark this year?

My chances are _____

❸ What is the **population** of your country?

The population is _____

❹ What news **report** would interest you?

I'd be interested in _____

Before You Listen

A. Look at this diagram of systems in the human body. Label the four systems: *circulation, muscle, nervous,* and *skeleton.*

The Human Body's Systems

_____ *circulation*

_____

_____

_____
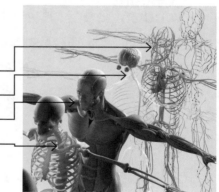

B. What's the function of each of the body's systems? How is each part important to athletes? Complete the table and then discuss with a partner.

SYSTEMS	FUNCTIONS	IMPORTANCE TO ATHLETES
circulation	*carries blood to muscles and organs*	
muscle		
nervous	*gives feedback and sends signals*	
skeleton		*structure (e.g., long legs for running)*

© ERPI • Reproduction prohibited

C. Think about professional athletes. Based on what you read so far and on the title of Listening 2 ("Human Physical Limits") predict what the listening will be about.

_____

_____

While You Listen

D. The first time you listen, try to understand the general idea. While you listen the second time, indicate the system, or systems, discussed in each segment. Listen a third time to check your answers.

SEGMENTS	CIRCULATION	MUSCLE	NERVOUS	SKELETON
❶ ... the story of Alex Kornaki ... is she a superhero?				
❷ I've heard stories of mothers saving their babies from danger like this ... comes from the adrenaline ...				
❸ As a coach, I've helped athletes chase records ... I started to wonder if we have reached our human limits.				
❹ Let's take the 100-metre sprint ... It doesn't seem like much.				
❺ I thought there would be a bigger difference ... and other sporting events as well.				
❻ Yes. The chart is titled, "Human Body's Systems" ... and other problems.				
❼ And the next part is ... gene ACTN3.				
❽ What's that ... Don't fight with a monkey!				
❾ Is the next part with the brain ... and other organs.				

After You Listen

E. Indicate whether these statements are true or false, according to the listening.

STATEMENTS	TRUE	FALSE
❶ Cora Mathews is a sports coach.		
❷ The story about Alex and Lauren Kornaki is about strength.		
❸ Babies can use hysterical strength to lift cars.		
❹ In a century, sprint records have only improved by ten seconds.		
❺ Better tracks and footwear have made a huge difference.		
❻ Lifting heavy weights can sometimes cause bone breakage.		
❼ ACTN3 is a gene found in most top runners.		
❽ It's likely that new sporting records will continue to be set.		

© ERPI • Reproduction prohibited

F. What is the main idea of Listening 2? Choose the best summary.

☐ With the help of hormones and adrenaline, it's likely that people will soon be strong enough to lift cars and run at high speeds.

☐ The body's systems work together to allow for high performance but there are likely limits to increases in strength and speed.

☐ No one can imagine how much faster people might be able to run or how much weight they may eventually be able to lift.

G. Check your answers in Before You Listen, tasks B and C. Is there anything you would change? Discuss with a partner.

FOCUS ON SPEAKING

Structuring a Presentation

When you give a presentation, you need a structure. A common structure is to explain a problem and then offer a solution. Here is an example of five steps you might follow to talk about a new habit or routine.

STEPS		EXPLANATIONS
❶	problem	Explain why people need to change something they do, or do something new.
❷	solution	Explain the solution: a new habit.
❸	skill	Define the habit and explain how it works.
❹	practice	Explain how to make the habit routine (done regularly).
❺	outcome	Explain what happens after the habit is adopted.

A. Listen to a short talk on how to be happy and write brief notes about each step.

STEPS		EXPLANATIONS
❶	problem	*people are unhappy*
❷	solution	
❸	skill	
❹	practice	
❺	outcome	

B. Use your notes to explain the "slice of joy habit" to a partner.

© **ERPI** • Reproduction prohibited

WARM-UP ASSIGNMENT
Talk about a Habit

Improving your mental and physical abilities often starts with developing new habits or routines. In this Warm-Up Assignment, you will choose a topic and talk about a new habit you think others should learn.

A. Choose a topic from Listening 1 or Listening 2. Consider the limits of a person's mental or physical abilities and decide on a new habit or routine that could help improve those abilities.

B. Use the five steps you learned in Focus on Speaking to structure your talk. Explain the problem and offer your solution. Write your notes in the table below.

STEPS	EXPLANATIONS
❶ problem	
❷ solution	
❸ skill	
❹ practice	
❺ outcome	

> ❶ Use feedback from your teacher and classmates on this Warm-Up Assignment to improve your speaking.

C. Practise your talk in front of a mirror. Then explain your new habit to a partner.

LISTENING ❸   How to Have a Good Day

Everyone has good days and bad days. But do some people have more bad days than others? Or is it just your way of looking at the world? What would it take for you to turn bad days into good days?

VOCABULARY BUILD

In the following exercises, explore key words from Listening 3.

A. Fill in the blanks with the correct words to complete the paragraph.

attitude	demands	opportunity	priority

A new exercise program always _____ a lot of your time. But regular exercise can be an _____ to get in better shape and feel better about who you are. You need to make it work by changing your _____, believing that you can make a change if you just try. Also, you need to make exercise a _____ and not be distracted by other people and events.

© **ERPI** • Reproduction prohibited

B. Match each noun to its definition.

NOUNS		DEFINITIONS
1 assumption	_____	a) something more important than others
2 priority	_____	b) the world as it actually exists
3 reaction	_____	c) something accepted as true
4 reality	_____	d) a response to a situation or event

C. What do the words in bold mean to you? Complete the sentences.

1 Who makes the most **demands** on your time?

The person is _____

2 What's your **reaction** when you get a lot of homework?

I feel _____

3 What is a **priority** for you to do every day?

Every day I _____

4 What **attitude** helps you get work done?

One attitude is _____

5 What's a **reality** of student life you didn't expect?

I never expected _____

My eLab ✎

Visit My eLab to complete Vocabulary Review exercises for this chapter.

Before You Listen

A. Listening 3 begins with a quote by Annie Dillard: "How we spend our days is, of course, how we spend our lives." Based on this quote, predict what this listening will be about.

_____

_____

B. The listening talks about people having two modes—or ways—of working and living. Read this excerpt and then write two experiences you had, good or bad. Were you in a defensive mode or in a discovery mode? Share your experiences with a partner.

> The core message that I gathered from her book is that we are always either in a defensive mode, or in a discovery mode. We go between this discovery mode, where we have clarity and we are seeking opportunity to advance our goals, to a defensive mode, where we are living in reaction to other people's demands, and we feel overwhelmed.

1 _____

_____

2 _____

_____

© ERPI • Reproduction prohibited

C. Listening 3 breaks the day into three sections and suggests that at waking time you want to be intentional, that is, sort out your plans. Write three things you would like to do today. What would help you do them? What would get in the way? Discuss your answers with a partner.

THREE THINGS TO DO	WHAT WOULD HELP	WHAT WOULD GET IN THE WAY
❶		
❷		
❸		

D. The listening also suggests there are three ways of setting intentions: *aim*, *attitude*, and *attention*. Here is how the terms are defined. Write an example from your own life for each.

TERMS	DEFINITIONS	EXAMPLES
aim	discovering the most important activities in your day	
attitude	asking yourself what matters most	
attention	ignoring people and things that might interrupt you	

While You Listen

E. The narrator draws images to illustrate what he is saying, to help make sense of the talk. The first time you listen, try to understand the general idea. While you listen the second time, write notes on the images and what is said about each one. Listen a third time to check your notes and add details.

funnel

clipboard

checklist

envelope

SEGMENTS	IMAGES	NOTES
❶ Welcome to another episode ... how to be most effective throughout the day.	*bad day / good day diagram*	• *Webb has analyzed what makes a good day and a bad day.*
❷ The core message that I gathered ...		• *we are in defensive or discovery mode* • *defensive:* _____ • *discovery:* _____

© ERPI • Reproduction prohibited

SEGMENTS	IMAGES	NOTES
❸ Each day we have a choice ...	*upset guy with the words "too much"*	• situations _____ • *adrenaline produced*
❹ The edgy state can feel exciting at first ...		• erodes _____
❺ Let's look at our day and break it up ...		• *three components*
❻ The brain is always filtering through large amounts of information ...		• we have to decide _____
❼ Think of your mind ...		•
❽ First we aim to discover the most important ...		•
❾ Take these one or two outcomes ...	*clipboard and calendar*	•
❿ Harvard Business School ...	*Harvard crest*	• people are more creative when they can _____
⓫ A study from Microsoft ...	*Microsoft logo*	• after interruptions, it takes fifteen minutes _____

After You Listen

F. Connect these phrases to create a summary of Listening 3.

SUMMARY		
❶ "How we spend our days is, of course, ...	_____	a) let the day happen to us.
❷ We can advance our goals or live ...	_____	b) schedule an uninterrupted block of time.
❸ We miss a big opportunity if we simply ...	_____	c) like a huge spam filter.
❹ The brain filters information ...	_____	d) when people were able to focus on one task.
❺ The things that get through the filters are strongly influenced ...	_____	e) how we spend our lives."
❻ We should find one or two clear outcomes and ...	_____	f) took fifteen minutes to fully regain their train of thought.
❼ A Harvard study found creative thinking was higher ...	_____	g) by priorities and assumptions.
❽ A Microsoft study found employees interrupted by email ...	_____	h) in reaction to other people's demands.

© ERPI • Reproduction prohibited

G. What do these ideas from Listening 3 mean to you? Write your answers and then discuss with a partner.

① "We can advance our goals or live in reaction to other people's demands." Write one of your goals and one demand you have from another person.

GOAL: _____

DEMAND: _____

_____

② "The things that get through the filters are strongly influenced by priorities and assumptions." Write one of your priorities and one of your assumptions.

PRIORITY: _____

ASSUMPTION: _____

_____

H. How should you structure your day? Number these steps in order, according to the listening.

_____ Choose one or two outcomes.

_____ List your wishes for actions to take, people to meet, and work to do.

_____ Schedule an uninterrupted block of time.

_____ Spend a few minutes thinking about your priorities and assumptions.

_____ Ask yourself what matters most to make this day successful.

_____ Wake up and be intentional.

I. What do you think is the intention of Listening 3? Write the main idea and then discuss with a partner.

_____

_____

_____

© ERPI • Reproduction prohibited

Academic
Survival Skill

Talking with Graphic Organizers

Since the 1940s, there has been a belief that we remember only 10 percent of what we read, but 50 percent of what we see and hear. Although the percentages are not true, the principle makes sense. Even for very short talks, it helps to have the support of a graphic organizer, which makes things easier to understand and more memorable.

A. Here are six strategies you can use to make a talk with graphic organizers more effective. For each strategy, note which you already do and which you should do.

PRESENTATION STRATEGIES		ALREADY DO	SHOULD DO
BEFORE YOU PRESENT	a) Think about the information you have to present. Ask how a graphic organizer supports it.		
	b) Edit the graphic organizer to ensure that it only includes the information your audience needs.		
WHILE YOU PRESENT	c) Choose when to show your graphic organizer; too early and your audience will look at it rather than listen to you.		
	d) Explain the graphic organizer in a way that is easy to follow. If it is too complicated, use more than one.		
AFTER YOU PRESENT	e) Ask the audience for questions. If they do not have any, ask them a question to make sure they understood your talk.		
	f) Review what was effective so that you can improve your graphic organizers and future talks.		

B. Read these problems. Write the letter of the strategy that would have solved each problem.

_____ He left his chart on the screen for the whole presentation. I read it long before he started explaining it.

_____ She made the same mistakes this time as the last time she presented.

_____ I don't think he spent any time thinking about the chart and how he would use it.

_____ He took too long. He should have finished early because I wanted to ask a question about the map he showed us.

_____ I found the bar chart confusing. She didn't even talk about half the things that were on it.

_____ Why didn't he spread the information over three charts? It would be easier to follow.

FINAL ASSIGNMENT
Discuss a New Habit

Use what you learned in this chapter to explain your new habit or routine to a small group.

A. Begin with the topic and the new habit you proposed in the Warm-Up Assignment (page 131). Based on the feedback you received, consider how you can improve your explanation.

B. Refer to what you learned in Focus on Speaking (page 130) to structure your talk. Prepare a graphic organizer to help explain your ideas.

© **ERPI** • Reproduction prohibited

C. Plan your presentation. Review the presentation strategies from Academic Survival Skill (page 135) so that you share your graphic organizer effectively and efficiently.

D. Form a small group. When it is your turn to speak, present your new habit. Begin by greeting your group and explaining what you will talk about. End by asking a comprehension question. When you finish, invite group members to ask questions.

Examples: Today, I'd like to tell you about …

Who can tell me … ?

Now, I'm happy to answer any questions about …

E. While you listen to the other group members' presentations, try to connect their graphic organizers to their ideas (see Focus on Listening, page 120).

F. When all group members have presented, ask and answer questions about each other's presentations.

Examples: Great presentation! I just wanted to ask about …

I understand … but I wasn't sure about …

In your graphic organizer you show … Could you explain in more detail, please?

G. After, in a group, review your presentations and the questions. Discuss what you each could have done better.

How confident are you?

Think about what you learned in this chapter. Use the table to decide what you should review. Share your answers with a partner.

I LEARNED …	I AM CONFIDENT	I NEED TO REVIEW
vocabulary related to physical and mental abilities;	☐	☐
to listen for details about charts;	☐	☐
to predict to listen effectively;	☐	☐
to use the present perfect tense;	☐	☐
how to structure a presentation;	☐	☐
how to talk with graphic organizers;	☐	☐
how to talk about a new habit and discuss it in a group.	☐	☐

My eLab ✎

Visit My eLab to build on what you learned.

CHAPTER 8

The Sixth Extinction

You spend most of your time thinking about small day-to-day problems. Large problems, like climate change, can seem too complex and not something you can do anything about. But climate change is becoming one threat that could make all other problems seem small in comparison. Climate change and other factors might eventually lead to a sixth extinction where people, like dinosaurs and other ancient creatures, disappear from Earth. What could you do to help stop the sixth extinction?

In this chapter,
you will

- learn vocabulary related to extinctions;

- listen for sequence;

- paraphrase to understand;

- review simple past and present perfect tenses;

- make and respond to suggestions;

- learn how to take part in a panel discussion;

- discuss an extinction event and share ideas in a panel discussion.

GEARING UP

A. Look at the illustration and then answer the questions.

1 The tree resembles a human organ. What organ is it shaped like?

_____

_____

2 Trees and other plants take carbon dioxide (CO_2) from the air and produce oxygen. Why do we need plants to do this?

_____

_____

3 Besides producing oxygen, what are other benefits of trees?

_____

_____

4 In some countries, large forests and jungles are set on fire to clear land for farming. Why is this a problem?

_____

_____

B. Discuss the questions and your answers, first with a partner, then in a group.

Below are the key words you will practise in this chapter. Check the words you understand and then underline the words you use.

These words are from the Longman Communication 3000 and the Academic Word List. See Appendix 2, page 158.

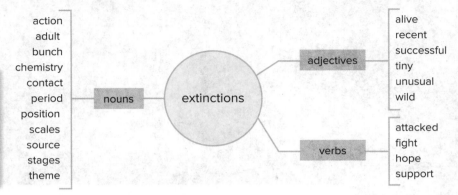

nouns (extinctions)
action
adult
bunch
chemistry
contact
period
position
scales
source
stages
theme

adjectives
alive
recent
successful
tiny
unusual
wild

verbs
attacked
fight
hope
support

FOCUS ON LISTENING

Listening for Sequence

You often listen to a sequence of events, such as when you hear someone tell a story. There is a clear beginning, middle, and end connected with transition words. Many times, a sequence is introduced with a question, beginning with the question word *how*. The words that follow answer the question by explaining the steps. Other times, a sequence is introduced with phrases that might include words like *happened, occurred, sequence, series,* and *steps.*

A. Listen to an explanation of how climate change can happen. Then put these phrases in order. The key words introducing the phrases are missing.

___1___ How does climate change happen in the first place?

_____ affected plants and animals on land

_____ can occur quickly or over hundreds or thousands of years

_____ carbon dioxide built up, it affected the oceans

_____ imagine there was a proper balance in oxygen and carbon dioxide levels

_____ wouldn't make a difference because the change in carbon dioxide was quite small

_____ made the oceans more acidic, fish and other marine animals died

_____ this has changed because of natural events, such as forest fires and volcanic eruptions

___9___ In the end, the change in carbon dioxide levels led to climate change.

When you listen to a sequence, you need to identify key words and phrases that tell you when each part of the sequence happened.

© ERPI • Reproduction prohibited

▶

B. Look at the five categories showing times in a sequence and example words. Complete the table with these words.

in the end	later	once	seldom	to begin

BEFORE	SOMETIMES	FIRST	NEXT	LAST
earlier	at times	at first	then	finally
in the past	from time to time	in the first place	after	at last

C. Listen to an excerpt from Listening 1. Identify the words and phrases used in the sequence and write them below.

1 *from time to time*   **3** _____   **5** _____

2 _____   **4** _____   **6** _____

FOCUS ON CRITICAL THINKING

Paraphrasing to Understand

Paraphrasing is explaining an idea in your own words. There are two reasons to paraphrase. The first is to take notes, breaking down complex ideas to make them easier to study. The second is to check your understanding. In a conversation, paraphrasing lets the speaker know you are listening and trying to understand. If your paraphrase is not correct, the speaker can try to explain a point in a better way. When you paraphrase in a conversation, use these strategies.

• Begin with a question that shows your paraphrase is to check understanding: *In other words, do you mean ... ? Are you saying ... ? Do I understand you correctly when ... ?*

• Focus on the main idea and simplify the content: take out examples and use simpler words.

• Listen to the response to your paraphrase. If you still don't understand, try paraphrasing in a new way. It's OK to ask the question once or twice, but then let the conversation continue and ask questions at the end.

A. Consider the main idea of each sentence and then choose the best paraphrase question.

1 There, the sailors encountered a new bird that was unable to fly, the dodo. By 1662, it had disappeared.

    a) So, are you saying that the sailors caused the dodo to go extinct?

    b) By this, do you mean that the dodo was unable to fly?

2 Wolves manage other species, like deer, by killing the sick and old ones.

    a) So, are you saying that you hate wolves because they kill deer?

    b) Do I understand you correctly when you say wolves have an important role in the wild?

© ERPI • Reproduction prohibited

3 Sometime between 1937 and 1950, habitat loss on Bali meant less jungle for the Bali tiger, and less support, in terms of the animals that tigers needed for food.

   a) Do you mean that other animals besides tigers have not suffered habitat loss on Bali?

   b) In other words, are you saying if there were more jungle, the tigers would still be there?

4 The last Pyrenean ibex, a kind of wild goat, is unusual because it went extinct twice: first in 2000 after humans caused climate change that affected the food supply, and again in 2009 after an ibex clone died.

dodo bird

   a) Am I hearing you correctly that cloning the ibex was unsuccessful?

   b) You're not saying that we shouldn't clone the Pyrenean ibex, are you?

LISTENING ❶   The Roads to Extinction

You will probably never see a live passenger pigeon, even though there were once billions of them in North America. Your grandchildren may never see a polar bear in the wild; polar bears are already a vulnerable species. Many animals will become extinct if we do not do more to protect them.

VOCABULARY BUILD

In the following exercises, explore key words from Listening 1.

A. Match each word to its antonym.

WORDS		ANTONYMS
❶ alive (adj.)	_____	a) protected
❷ attacked (v.)	_____	b) common
❸ support (v.)	_____	c) tame
❹ unusual (adj.)	_____	d) dead
❺ wild (adj.)	_____	e) oppose

B. The words *source, stages,* and *support* can be used as nouns or verbs. Fill in the blanks to complete the sentences.

  ❶ From childhood to old age, we all go through different _____ in life.

  ❷ We are trying to _____ genetic material from animals in zoos.

© **ERPI** • Reproduction prohibited

3 There are many reasons to _____ groups opposed to climate change.

4 The group _____ a protest each time another animal goes extinct.

5 I need to find _____ for my opinions about extinction.

6 As their main _____ of food disappeared, so did the mammoths.

C. What do the words in bold mean to you? Complete the sentences.

1 What is one **unusual** habit you have?

One habit is _____

2 What is one **wild** idea you have?

One idea is _____

3 How do you describe your **stage** of life?

I'm _____

4 What's the **source** of the news you read or hear?

My news source is _____

Before You Listen

A. Look at the collage of sixteen creatures. Circle the ones you can name. Choose one that you think is likely to go extinct and explain why. Choose one that you think is unlikely to go extinct and explain why.

LIKELY TO GO EXTINCT: _____

WHY: _____

_____

UNLIKELY TO GO EXTINCT: _____

WHY: _____

_____

While You Listen

B. The first time you listen, try to understand the general idea. While you listen a second time, paraphrase the reason each creature went extinct and write the speaker's suggestions for saving each one. Listen a third time to check your notes and add details.

CREATURES	REASONS EACH WENT EXTINCT	SUGGESTIONS FOR SAVING THEM
dodo	*hunted for food and rats ate the dodo's eggs*	
Newfoundland wolf		
passenger pigeon		
Bali tiger		*create a wildlife refuge*
Pyrenean ibex		

© **ERPI** • Reproduction prohibited

After You Listen

C. Choose the phrase that best completes each sentence, according to the listening.

1 Something all the creatures in Listening 1 have in common is that they _____.

a) have mostly been brought back

b) died as a result of human actions

c) were no longer useful to people

2 The time machine idea allows Dr. Mendel to suggest _____.

a) how to imagine a new future

b) things no one wants to hear

c) ideas for people in the past

3 The story about the rats suggests there were no rats _____.

a) on Mauritius before the Dutch came

b) big enough to eat a dodo egg

c) on the Dutch ships after they landed

4 The Newfoundland wolf ate animals that _____.

a) farmers didn't need

b) farmers needed

c) were only found in the wild

5 The passenger pigeon was probably in a zoo because people _____.

a) realized the species was disappearing

b) were afraid the bird might fly away

c) were no longer afraid of the birds

6 The dates from 1937 to 1950 suggest people don't really know _____.

a) about calendars in some countries

b) when the last Bali tiger died

c) how many tigers there once were

passenger pigeon

D. Based on what you understand from the listening, and the sequence words you learned in Focus on Listening (page 140), number these points in order.

_____ After, the Europeans hunted the passenger pigeons, first for food, then for sport.

_____ Before Europeans had arrived in North America, passenger pigeons grew in number.

_____ Finally, the last passenger pigeon died and the species went extinct.

_____ In the end, only one passenger pigeon was left, in a zoo.

_____ Soon, the Europeans began to farm. The passenger pigeons may have damaged some crops.

© ERPI • Reproduction prohibited

E. Dr. Mendel's time machine is fiction. But, if you could go back in time and save one species in Listening 1, which one would it be? Why? Discuss your choice with a partner.

I would save _____ because _____

_____

FOCUS ON GRAMMAR

Simple Past and Present Perfect

You use the simple past and present perfect tenses to talk about things that have happened. Look at this table to learn the rules for when to use each one.

SIMPLE PAST	PRESENT PERFECT
Finished actions Example: He **visited** three museums **last year**.	Actions that started in the past and continue in the present Example: He **has visited** three **museums this year**.
Actions that happened at a specified time Example: I **saw** her **last Saturday**.	Actions that happened at an unspecified time Example: I **haven't seen** her **for a long time**.

A. Complete these sentences. Fill in the blanks with the correct form of the verbs in parentheses: simple past or present perfect. Use the negative form where indicated.

① I (be) _____ on a research trip for a month last year.

② You (get, negative) _____ your final grades.

③ He (work) _____ on a farm for several years.

④ We (visit) _____ a forest last Tuesday.

⑤ She (see, negative) _____ him today.

⑥ They (eat) _____ lunch at noon.

B. Often the simple past tense and the present progressive tense are combined in one sentence. Complete each sentence with the simple past or present perfect form of the verb in parentheses.

① She has studied climate change for years and she (write) _____ a book about it.

② Her book came out last month and (sell) _____ well.

③ So far, she has travelled to three countries to promote it and, of the three, she (like) _____ Italy best.

④ She (plan) _____ a vacation after she finishes her travels.

⑤ Critics have said she (do) _____ a good job.

⑥ Both she and her editor enjoyed working on the book and they (plan) _____ to work on another.

My eLab 🖊

Visit My eLab to complete Grammar Review exercises for this chapter.

Dinosaurs Around Us

Countless plants and animals have become extinct. What if we could bring extinct creatures back? It's becoming increasingly possible. But in the movie *Jurassic Park*, about a theme park with dinosaurs, one character observes: "Scientists were so preoccupied with whether or not they *could*, they didn't stop to think if they *should*." Should we bring back dinosaurs and other extinct creatures?

VOCABULARY BUILD

In the following exercises, explore key words from Listening 2.

A. Draw an arrow ↓ to indicate where the word in parentheses should be placed in each sentence.

① (action) The of mammoth feet broke up the earth .

② (theme) I'd like to suggest that it's a common of science fiction .

③ (fight) Imagine a mammoth wanted to start a with you .

④ (hope) Let's that doesn't happen .

⑤ (scales) If scientists changed feathers to , we could find ourselves surrounded by little dinosaurs .

B. Match each word to its synonym.

WORDS		SYNONYMS
① adult (n.)	_____	a) believe
② fight (v.)	_____	b) idea
③ hope (v.)	_____	c) grown-up
④ successful (adj.)	_____	d) struggle
⑤ theme (n.)	_____	e) doing well

C. What do the words in bold mean to you? Complete the sentences.

① What's something you **hope** will happen?

I hope _____

② What would make you feel **successful**?

I'd feel successful _____

③ What makes you feel like an **adult**?

I feel like an adult _____

④ What is a cause you would **fight** for?

I'd fight _____

© **ERPI** • Reproduction prohibited

⑤ Which one **action** would improve your local environment?

One action is _____

Before You Listen

A. Read this excerpt from Listening 2. Write what you think would be the advantages and disadvantages to bringing back long-extinct creatures. Then discuss your answers with a partner.

> Writer Michael Crichton is perhaps best known for his 1990 novel, *Jurassic Park*. In the novel, and the movie made from it, scientists extracted DNA from the blood of ancient mosquitoes and used it to clone dinosaurs. They succeeded in bringing sixty-five-million-year-old monsters back to life. It turned out badly for the humans.

EXTINCT CREATURES	ADVANTAGES TO BRINGING IT BACK	DISADVANTAGES TO BRINGING IT BACK
dinosaur	*high interest from the public*	
mammoth		

B. If you could bring back an extinct creature, which qualities would you want the creatures to have? Discuss your reasons with a partner.

☐ cute   ☐ makes a good pet
☐ eats pests   ☐ recently disappeared
☐ friendly   ☐ useful as farm animals
☐ intelligent   ☐ useful food source

While You Listen

C. The first time you listen, try to understand the general idea. While you listen the second time, paraphrase the five criteria. Listen a third time to check the criteria and to indicate whether dinosaurs or mammoths fit each criterion.

CRITERIA	DINOSAURS	MAMMOTHS
CRITERION 1:	*no*	
CRITERION 2:		
CRITERION 3:		
CRITERION 4:		
CRITERION 5:		

© **ERPI** • Reproduction prohibited

After You Listen

D. Choose the word or phrase that best completes each sentence, according to the listening.

1. The idea of meddling (interfering) with things we don't understand has to do with _____.

   a) old experiments   b) winning prizes   c) cloning

2. The idea behind de-extinction is to _____ animals that have disappeared.

   a) bring back   b) hunt for   c) create farm

3. A big question is whether an extinct animal would _____ in today's world.

   a) be hungry   b) freeze   c) fit

4. Today's closest relatives to dinosaurs are _____.

   a) alligators

   b) birds

   c) snakes

5. The speaker suggests we _____ want little dinosaurs.

   a) wouldn't

   b) would

   c) might

6. Mammoths walked Earth as recently as _____ years ago.

   a) four thousand

   b) forty thousand

   c) sixty-five million

7. Mammoths might make the land _____.

   a) more dangerous   b) wetter   c) more productive

8. One theory suggests _____ made the mammoths extinct.

   a) poison plants   b) human hunters   c) dinosaurs

E. Number these steps in sequence to explain how to clone a mammoth.

_____ Collect the mammoth's living cells.

_____ Introduce the baby mammoth into the wild.

_____ Find a frozen mammoth.

_____ Insert the cells into elephant eggs.

_____ Help the mammoth make the land more productive.

_____ Wait two years for the mammoth to be born.

© ERPI • Reproduction prohibited

F. Scientists are interested in the de-extinction of animals that disappeared thousands or millions of years ago. But other animals are becoming extinct today. Should scientists be more focused on animals threatened with extinction today? Why or why not? Discuss with a partner.

FOCUS ON SPEAKING

It's polite to phrase suggestions as questions.

Making and Responding to Suggestions

A suggestion is an idea you share to help make something better. When you hear someone explain a problem, you may offer a suggestion to help solve it. Or, you may offer a suggestion during (or after) a presentation to help the speaker improve. Sometimes a speaker invites suggestions: "What would you suggest?" But only offer suggestions when they are welcome; a person who is not looking for a suggestion is unlikely to appreciate one. Use these expressions when you want to make suggestions.

- How about … ?
- Why don't you … ?
- What about … ?
- Do you think you should … ?

A. Read these problems, and using the phrases above, complete the suggestions.

1 You were speaking a bit too fast.

_____How about_____ slowing down a little?

2 I couldn't see your graphic organizer.

_____ make it bigger?

3 The room is too big and I couldn't hear you.

_____ speak louder?

4 I didn't understand the example you gave.

_____ giving another one?

5 The sequence you described wasn't clear.

_____ using numbers?

B. Work with a partner. Discuss each problem below. Then take turns offering suggestions on what could be done to help solve them.

a) An asteroid may impact (hit) Earth, like the one that led to the death of the dinosaurs sixty-five million years ago.

b) We're changing the climate more rapidly than many species can adapt.

c) Ships and planes carry different insects, marine life, and other creatures to other parts of the world where they may damage the environment.

© ERPI • Reproduction prohibited

WARM-UP ASSIGNMENT

Discuss an Extinction Event

In this Warm-Up Assignment, you will choose an extinct creature, paraphrase what you know about it, and explain the problems it might cause if it came back today in large numbers.

A. Listenings 1 and 2 talked about extinctions. Listening 1 looked at the reasons for the extinctions of the dodo bird, the Newfoundland wolf, the passenger pigeon, the Bali tiger, and the Pyrenean ibex. Listening 2 looked at the extinction of dinosaurs and mammoths and at attempts to bring them back. Choose one of these creatures.

B. Paraphrase what you know about the creature in your own words.

Example: The dodo was a bird that couldn't fly and couldn't escape from human hunters and egg-eating rats.

Use feedback from your teacher and classmates on this Warm-Up Assignment to improve your speaking.

C. Imagine your creature has come back. Make a list of any problems the creature might cause. For example, some creatures might hunt other animals, or even people.

D. Discuss your creature with a partner. Talk about the problems your listed. Use what you learned in Focus on Speaking to make suggestions about what could be done.

Academic
Survival Skill

Pronunciation: The "-ed" ending can be pronounced in three ways: "Id" in words like invited; "t" in words like talked; and "d" in words like used.

My eLab

Visit My eLab to complete a pronunciation exercise.

Taking Part in a Panel Discussion

There are many kinds of meetings, each with different purposes. A panel discussion is a meeting that is often used to explore issues. Panellists, who are experts, are invited to share their ideas. A moderator is in charge of the meeting and acts like a referee giving turns and indicating when a panellist has talked enough. Here is the way most panel discussions are conducted.

- To begin, the moderator welcomes the audience and explains the topic of the panel discussion.

- Next, the panellists are introduced or asked to introduce themselves, giving their names and other key information such as what makes them experts on the topic.

- After the introductions, each panellist gives initial comments. If the panel discussion is about a topic that is *for* or *against* something, panellists may briefly explain their point of view.

- From time to time, the moderator asks panellists to answer questions.

© ERPI • Reproduction prohibited

- When the panellists finish their discussion, the audience may ask questions.
- At the end, the moderator may summarize the panel discussion before thanking the panellists and the audience.

A. Read this excerpt from Listening 3. Then write the two purposes for this introduction.

> **NEWS ANCHOR 1:** A new book finds humans are fundamentally changing our planet—and not for the better. It says that thousands of animals and plants are headed toward their demise. Elizabeth Kolbert is a journalist and the author of *The Sixth Extinction*. She joins us along with CBS This Morning contributor Michio Kaku, who's a professor at the City College of New York. Welcome.

PURPOSE 1: _____

PURPOSE 2: _____

B. Match each step to a comment. Then practise saying the comments with a partner.

STEPS		COMMENTS
❶ welcome the audience	_____	a) Our topic today is about the connections between extinctions and climate change.
❷ explain the topic	_____	b) Now, perhaps the audience has some questions.
❸ introduce the panellists	_____	c) Could you start by answering the question: "What is climate change?"
❹ panellists are asked to give initial comments	_____	d) We all agree something needs to be done about climate change. Thank you, everyone.
❺ panellists are asked to answer questions	_____	e) Welcome to today's panel discussion on extinctions.
❻ invite the audience to ask the panellists questions	_____	f) Before we start the discussion, could you each tell me the creature you're concerned about?
❼ summarize, and thank the panellists	_____	g) Today, our panellists are _____ and _____.

LISTENING ❸ **The Sixth Extinction**

Since the beginning of time, there have been five mass extinctions on Earth—five times when more than 75 percent of life was destroyed and what remained had to start evolving again. This has meant evolution followed different paths. The asteroid that struck Earth sixty-five million years ago wiped out the last dinosaurs. That event allowed small mammals to evolve into people. But now people, not an asteroid, may be the greatest threat to Earth. What should we do about it?

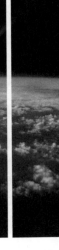

© **ERPI** • Reproduction prohibited

In the following exercises, explore key words from Listening 3.

A. Fill in the blanks with the correct words to complete the paragraph.

chemistry	contact	period	position	recent

A hundred years ago, _____ and biology were separate sciences, but in _____ times, there is more _____ between the two fields. This is in part because new tools allow biologists to study plants and animals at the cell level and even look into the chemical properties of their DNA. We are in a _____ where we are beginning to understand how we can change the DNA of plants and animals. Someone considering a _____ in this new field is likely to make important discoveries.

B. Words that are frequently used together are called *collocations*. Look at the key words and phrases. Cross out the word in each line that does not belong.

1. bunch of: flowers / people / balloons / grapes / many
2. chemistry: biology / textbook / class / lab / experiment
3. period of: time / stop / remembering / regret / revolution
4. recent: time / notice / soon / event / idea
5. tiny: gone / things / sounds / babies

C. What do the words in bold mean to you? Complete the sentences.

1. What is a **tiny** thing that sometimes surprises you?

   One thing is _____

   _____

2. What's a **recent** event you attended?

   I attended _____

   _____

3. Who is your **contact** in case of an emergency?

   My contact is _____

   _____

4. What **position** would you want in a government?

   I'd like to be _____

5. What other **period** of history do you wish you lived in? Why?

   I wish _____

   _____

My eLab ✎

Visit My eLab to complete Vocabulary Review exercises for this chapter.

© **ERPI** • Reproduction prohibited

Before You Listen

A. As already mentioned, there have been five mass extinctions when more than 75 percent of species disappeared, such as during the Late Devonian, when trilobites were the most common creatures. Read about the extinctions. Then answer the questions that follow.

trilobite

PERIODS	MILLIONS OF YEARS AGO	SPECIES LOSS	CAUSES
Ordovician	450–440	86 percent	ice age
Late Devonian	375–360	75 percent	land plants took oxygen from the water killing trilobites
Permian The Great Dying	251	96 percent	volcanoes exploded and added too much CO_2 to the atmosphere
Triassic	205	80 percent	no clear cause
Cretaceous	65	76 percent	volcanic activity, climate change, asteroid impact

❶ Why would an ice age lead to extinctions?

_____

❷ What causes of extinctions can humans *not* prevent?

_____

❸ What causes of extinctions can humans prevent?

_____

B. These phrases are from Listening 3. Match each to its explanation.

PHRASES		EXPLANATIONS
❶ headed toward their demise	_____	a) water ships use to stay steady
❷ rules of the game changed	_____	b) things that produce oxygen and consume carbon dioxide
❸ scientific consensus	_____	c) things are happening in a new way
❹ ballast water	_____	d) about to die
❺ lungs of Earth	_____	e) lower the impact
❻ mitigate the effects	_____	f) agreement among scientists

C. Listening 3 suggests that humans will cause the next mass extinction—the sixth—and that humans will be the ones to disappear. How could humans cause the next extinction? Write notes and then discuss with a partner.

_____

_____

© ERPI • Reproduction prohibited

While You Listen

D. The first time you listen, try to understand the general idea. While you listen the second time, complete the paraphrases of the key ideas. Listen a third time to check your notes and add details.

Pyrenean ibex

INTERVIEWERS' QUESTIONS	EXPERTS' ANSWERS
❶ NEWS ANCHOR 1: So when I was going through the book …	**KOLBERT:** *We've learned that the rules of the game changed so you don't know what's going to happen.*
❷ NEWS ANCHOR 1: Are you predicting something catastrophic?	**KOLBERT:** • scientists believe _____ _____ • now humans are _____ _____
❸ NEWS ANCHOR 2: Just for the record, what are the other five great extinctions?	**KOLBERT:** • over the last _____ • Cretaceous, about _____
❹ NEWS ANCHOR 2: Did it, was it instant or did they die off over a period of time?	**KOLBERT:** • everything compressed down to a layer; difficult to know _____
❺ NEWS ANCHOR 2: But what are you really saying here?	**KOLBERT:** • rapid change means animals _____ • we're changing the climate by putting carbon dioxide into the _____ • moving things around the planet, e.g., in ships' ballast water: _____
❻ NEWS ANCHOR 1: So, Professor Kaku, when you hear that, do you think, "We need to do something, and we need to do it now?"	**KAKU:** • Why care about _____ _____ • Humans are at the top of the food chain. And it wouldn't take much to topple us. • oceans more acidified because of _____ _____ • a die-off in the _____ _____

© **ERPI** • Reproduction prohibited

▶

INTERVIEWERS' QUESTIONS	EXPERTS' ANSWERS
	• oxygen, carbon dioxide gets cycled _____ _____ • As we deforest the rainforest, we endanger our air. • The next endangered species could be _____
❼ **NEWS ANCHOR 1:** Deforest a rainforest, you mean cutting down the trees. The carbon dioxide that we're putting in the air is destroying the coral reefs.	**KAKU:** • the rise and fall of _____ • *Mayan, Anasazi, Easter Islanders* • all declined because _____ _____
❽ **NEWS ANCHOR 3:** But Elizabeth, this is reversible?	**KOLBERT:** • _____ • Question: *What are we going to do, now? Can we mitigate the effects?* • Yes, e.g., less _____

After You Listen

E. Indicate whether these statements are true or false, according to the listening.

STATEMENTS	TRUE	FALSE
❶ The last mass extinction happened sixty-five million years ago.		
❷ Humans have not fundamentally changed the planet.		
❸ The rules of the survival game have not changed.		
❹ Animals are in trouble when there is a rapid change in climate.		
❺ Too much CO_2 in the air and oceans may lead to humans going extinct.		
❻ The Mayans, Anasazi, and Easter Islanders were all killed by asteroids.		

Easter Island Statues

F. Number these points in the correct sequence.

_____ a die-off in the coral reefs

_____ as we deforest the rainforest, we're endangering the air we breathe

_____ a die-off in the fish population

_____ carbon dioxide gets cycled through the Amazon rainforest

_____ next endangered species could be us

_____ oceans become more acidified because of acid rain from coal plants, carbon dioxide in the atmosphere

FINAL ASSIGNMENT

Share Ideas in a Panel Discussion

Imagine that long-extinct creatures have returned to the modern world in great numbers. Use what you learned in this chapter to share ideas and make suggestions in an emergency panel discussion.

A. Based on the feedback you received on your Warm-Up Assignment, consider how you can improve your presentation.

B. Review what you learned in Academic Survival Skill (page 150) about how a panel discussion is conducted. Form groups of six. One student acts as moderator.

C. When you have been introduced, use the information from your Warm-Up Assignment to give initial comments about your creature and the problems its return has caused.

D. During the discussion, both the moderator and the panellists may ask questions.

E. Listen to other panellists and offer suggestions about what could be done (see Focus on Speaking, page 149).

F. After, review your presentations and suggestions and think about what you could improve.

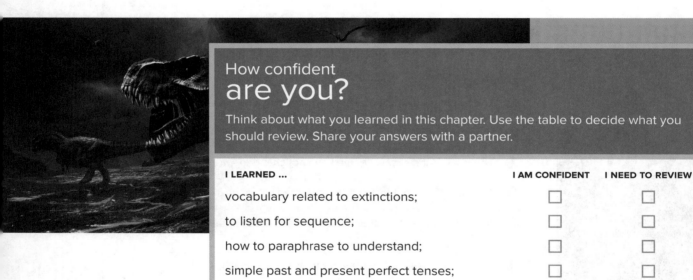

How confident are you?

Think about what you learned in this chapter. Use the table to decide what you should review. Share your answers with a partner.

I LEARNED ...	I AM CONFIDENT	I NEED TO REVIEW
vocabulary related to extinctions;	☐	☐
to listen for sequence;	☐	☐
how to paraphrase to understand;	☐	☐
simple past and present perfect tenses;	☐	☐
how to make and respond to suggestions;	☐	☐
how to take part in a panel discussion;	☐	☐
to discuss an extinction event and share ideas in a panel discussion.	☐	☐

My eLab

Visit My eLab to build on what you learned.

© ERPI • Reproduction prohibited

APPENDIX 1
Pronunciation Guide

	VOWELS						
IPA	**EXAMPLES**	**IPA**	**EXAMPLES**	**IPA**	**EXAMPLES**	**IPA**	**EXAMPLES**
ʌ	cup, luck	ɜ:	turn, learn	ʊ	put, could	eə	where, air
ɑ:	arm, father	ɪ	hit, sitting	u:	blue, food	eɪ	say, eight
æ	cat, black	i:	see, heat	aɪ	five, eye	ɪə	near, here
e	met, bed	ɒ	hot, rock	aʊ	now, out	ɔɪ	boy, join
ə	away, cinema	ɔ:	call, four	oʊ	go, home	ʊə	pure, tourist

	CONSONANTS				
IPA	**EXAMPLES**	**IPA**	**EXAMPLES**	**IPA**	**EXAMPLES**
b	bad, lab	m	man, lemon	tʃ	check, church
d	did, lady	n	no, ten	θ	think, both
f	find, if	ŋ	sing, finger	ð	this, mother
g	give, flag	p	pet, map	v	voice, five
h	how, hello	r	red, try	w	wet, window
j	yes, yellow	s	sun, miss	z	zoo, lazy
k	cat, black	ʃ	she, crash	ʒ	pleasure, vision
l	leg, little	t	tea, getting	dʒ	just, large

© **ERPI** • Reproduction prohibited

APPENDIX 2 Vocabulary

S1: one of the 1000 most frequent words in spoken English
S2: one of the next 1000 most frequent words (1000–2000)
S3: one of the next 1000 most frequent words (2000–3000)
AWL: on the Academic Word List

A

access (n.)	Chap. 2: S2	AWL
account (n.)	Chap. 7: S1	
action (n.)	Chap. 8: S1	
actually (adv.)	Chap. 3: S1	
adult (n.)	Chap. 8: S2	AWL
advance (n.)	Chap. 7: S2	
aim (v.)	Chap. 1: S2	
alive (adj.)	Chap. 8: S2	
appeal (n.)	Chap. 5: S2	
appreciate (v.)	Chap. 7: S2	AWL
assumption (n.)	Chap. 7: S2	AWL
attacked (v.)	Chap. 8: S3	
attend (v.)	Chap. 4: S2	
attention (n.)	Chap. 2: S2	
attitude (n.)	Chap. 7: S2	AWL
available (adj.)	Chap. 3: S1	AWL
average (adj.)	Chap. 5: S2	

B

based (v.)	Chap. 1: S1	
basically (adv.)	Chap. 4: S1	
basis (n.)	Chap. 5: S2	
beginning (n.)	Chap. 2: S1	
benefits (n.)	Chap. 4: S2	AWL
briefly (adv.)	Chap. 7: S2	AWL
bunch (n.)	Chap. 8: S2	

C

cases (n.)	Chap. 1: S1	
centuries (n.)	Chap. 2: S2	
certain (adj.)	Chap. 1: S1	
certainly (adv.)	Chap. 6: S1	
challenge (n.)	Chap. 3: S2	AWL
chances (n.)	Chap. 7: S1	
chemistry (n.)	Chap. 8: S2	AWL
collect (v.)	Chap. 4: S1	
comfortable (adj.)	Chap. 1: S2	
common (adj.)	Chap. 2: S1	
communities (n.)	Chap. 3: S1	AWL
completed (v.)	Chap. 2: S2	
connected (v.)	Chap. 5: S2	
consider (v.)	Chap. 3: S1	
contact (n.)	Chap. 8: S2	AWL
continue (v.)	Chap. 2: S1	
cope (v.)	Chap. 7: S2	
current (adj.)	Chap. 2: S2	AWL
currently (adv.)	Chap. 7: S2	AWL

D

danger (n.)	Chap. 4: S2	
debate (v.)	Chap. 4: S2	AWL
decision (n.)	Chap. 6: S1	
defence (n.)	Chap. 6: S2	AWL
demands (n.)	Chap. 7: S2	
depending (v.)	Chap. 5: S1	
designed (v.)	Chap. 3: S3	AWL
designs (n.)	Chap. 2: S2	AWL
detail (n.)	Chap. 1: S2	
disappear (v.)	Chap. 6: S2	
doubt (n.)	Chap. 1: S1	

E

economic (adj.)	Chap. 6: S2	AWL
edge (n.)	Chap. 2: S2	
encourage (v.)	Chap. 6: S2	
enormous (adj.)	Chap. 3: S2	AWL
exist (v.)	Chap. 4: S2	
expect (v.)	Chap. 3: S1	
experience (v.)	Chap. 4: S2	
express (v.)	Chap. 1: S2	
extremely (adv.)	Chap. 5: S2	

F

fight (v.)	Chap. 8: S1	
flat (adj.)	Chap. 5: S2	

H

hard (adj.)	Chap. 1: S1	
height (n.)	Chap. 6: S2	
highly (adv.)	Chap. 2: S2	
hope (v.)	Chap. 8: S1	

I

ignore (v.)	Chap. 1: S2	AWL
impossible (adj.)	Chap. 4: S2	
include (v.)	Chap. 5: S1	
independent (adj.)	Chap. 5: S2	
individuals (n.)	Chap. 3: S2	AWL
instead (adv.)	Chap. 4: S1	
intend (v.)	Chap. 4: S2	
interest (n.)	Chap. 5: S1	
interested (adj.)	Chap. 1: S1	
interview (n.)	Chap. 1: S2	
introduce (v.)	Chap. 1: S2	
invited (v.)	Chap. 4: S2	

© ERPI • Reproduction prohibited

L

labour (n.)	Chap. 6: S2	AWL
lead (v.)	Chap. 6: S1	
lift (v.)	Chap. 7: S2	
limits (n.)	Chap. 7: S2	
local (adj.)	Chap. 3: S1	

M

managing (v.)	Chap. 6: S1	
master (n.)	Chap. 6: S2	
material (n.)	Chap. 2: S1	
mean (v.)	Chap. 4: S1	
mentioned (v.)	Chap. 4: S1	
methods (n.)	Chap. 5: S1	AWL
model (n.)	Chap. 5: S2	
modern (adj.)	Chap. 6: S1	

O

obviously (adv.)	Chap. 7: S1	AWL
occurred (v.)	Chap. 4: S1	AWL
operates (v.)	Chap. 7: S2	
opportunity (n.)	Chap. 7: S1	
opposite (adj.)	Chap. 1: S2	
original (adj.)	Chap. 2: S1	

P

particular (adj.)	Chap. 6: S1	
pattern (n.)	Chap. 5: S2	
perfectly (adv.)	Chap. 7: S2	
performance (n.)	Chap. 2: S2	
period (n.)	Chap. 8: S1	AWL
permanent (adj.)	Chap. 5: S2	
point (n.)	Chap. 1: S1	
political (adj.)	Chap. 6: S2	
popular (adj.)	Chap. 2: S2	
population (n.)	Chap. 7: S2	
position (n.)	Chap. 8: S1	
possible (adj.)	Chap. 1: S1	
previous (adj.)	Chap. 2: S1	AWL
principle (n.)	Chap. 3: S2	AWL
priority (n.)	Chap. 7: S2	AWL
private (adj.)	Chap. 5: S1	
probably (adv.)	Chap. 4: S1	
produced (v.)	Chap. 5: S1	
progress (n.)	Chap. 6: S2	
purpose (n.)	Chap. 2: S2	

Q

quote (v.)	Chap. 4: S2	AWL

R

rated (v.)	Chap. 3: S1	
reaction (n.)	Chap. 7: S2	AWL
reality (n.)	Chap. 7: S2	
recent (adj.)	Chap. 8: S2	
recommend (v.)	Chap. 3: S2	
record (n.)	Chap. 2: S1	
reduces (v.)	Chap. 5: S1	
regular (adj.)	Chap. 6: S2	
regulation (n.)	Chap. 3: S2	AWL
related (adj.)	Chap. 1: S2	
relationships (n.)	Chap. 3: S1	
release (v.)	Chap. 4: S2	AWL
relevant (adj.)	Chap. 3: S2	AWL
reports (n.)	Chap. 7: S2	
requires (v.)	Chap. 6: S1	AWL
research (n.)	Chap. 3: S2	AWL
respect (v.)	Chap. 1: S1	
responsibilities (n.)	Chap. 6: S2	
result (n.)	Chap. 5: S1	

S

scales (n.)	Chap. 8: S2	
select (v.)	Chap. 3: S2	AWL
separates (v.)	Chap. 4: S2	
services (n.)	Chap. 5: S1	
signal (n.)	Chap. 2: S2	
similar (adj.)	Chap. 3: S1	AWL
situation (n.)	Chap. 1: S1	
social (adj.)	Chap. 1: S1	
source (n.)	Chap. 8: S2	AWL
stages (n.)	Chap. 8: S1	
successful (adj.)	Chap. 8: S2	
suggest (v.)	Chap. 4: S1	
support (v.)	Chap. 8: S1	
surprised (adj.)	Chap. 1: S2	
survey (n.)	Chap. 3: S2	AWL
survive (v.)	Chap. 4: S2	AWL
systems (n.)	Chap. 2: S1	

T

tend (v.)	Chap. 5: S1	
theme (n.)	Chap. 8: S2	AWL
tiny (adj.)	Chap. 8: S2	
tremendous (adj.)	Chap. 6: S2	

U

unusual (adj.)	Chap. 8: S2	

V

vehicle (n.)	Chap. 3: S2	AWL
virtually (adv.)	Chap. 5: S2	AWL
voice (n.)	Chap. 6: S2	

W

waste (v.)	Chap. 3: S2	
weird (adj.)	Chap. 6: S2	
wild (adj.)	Chap. 8: S2	
wonder (v.)	Chap. 2: S1	

© ERPI • Reproduction prohibited

APPENDIX 3 Strategies for Improving Listening and Speaking Skills

1. Listening is made up of understanding the sounds and meanings of words as well as the pronunciation patterns of words, phrases, and sentences. **In your spare time, take the opportunity to listen to podcasts in your field of study as well as recordings of short stories and novels.** Listen several times, first to get the gist and the general patterns of pronunciation, then to understand new vocabulary in context. While you listen, try pronouncing portions of what you are hearing.

2. When you listen, you acquire new vocabulary, new ideas, and new ways of saying things. Research shows that simply listening to a lecture will lead to limited acquisition. Instead, you need to activate what you have heard by taking notes, reviewing them, and trying to use the language in other contexts, such as in a discussion with a study partner. The most effective way of learning new ideas is to teach. **Take what you've heard in a lecture, organize it, and share it with another person.** In this way, you are more likely to remember new words, expressions, and ideas.

3. **Whenever you listen, remind yourself of your purpose.** In some cases, you may listen passively, not bothering to remember most of the information you hear. For example, if you are in an airport, you will hear hundreds of announcements but only need to worry about those related to your flight. In other cases, you need to listen actively, measuring each idea you hear in terms of what it means to you. You might listen to understand, to summarize, to make a decision, or for other purposes. Knowing the purpose helps you focus on what to listen for.

4. **Interrupting is a key part of listening.** When you are in a conversation, one of the simplest and most basic ways to interrupt is to appear confused or frown. The other speaker will often take this as a cue to pause and explain in greater detail. Otherwise, stop the other speaker and politely ask for clarification. The speaker may repeat what was said, paraphrase the idea, provide an explanation, or give an example. If the clarification satisfies you, smile and nod. If not, ask questions to help you better understand.

5. **Listening strategies include top-down and bottom-up approaches.** In a *top-down* approach, you listen to predict what the talk will be about (based on your background knowledge), to identify the main idea, to draw inferences (guesses based on the facts), and to summarize ideas. In a *bottom-up* approach, you tend to listen for specific information, such as key words, directions, or instructions. In bottom-up listening, the main idea is not as important and you can't necessarily summarize the ideas effectively. Understanding why you are listening helps you choose between top-down and bottom-up approaches.

© **ERPI** • Reproduction prohibited

6 When you speak, you often end up repeating certain questions, answers, and statements. For example, you may ask questions when you meet someone new, provide answers about yourself, and make statements about everything from the weather to the latest news. For both informal and formal situations, practise these conversations in your head and say them out loud, adding details that help make you seem friendlier. **Find opportunities to speak.** For example, try engaging in short conversations in English with other commuters or people where you study or work.

7 You might not speak as much as you would like to because you become nervous in classroom conversations or social situations where you have to speak in front of a group of people. In these situations, you might feel that you cannot express yourself properly, perhaps because you cannot grasp the right words or keep up with what others are saying. But it's better to try and sometimes fail than to avoid speaking more than necessary. **Practising speaking is the key way to improve your speaking skills.**

8 **In academic situations where you need to make a presentation in front of a class, spend as much time as possible on preparation, rehearsing what you have to say until it feels conversational.** Don't memorize it but speak as though you are explaining the ideas in a relaxed way to a close friend for the first time. Use confident body language and maintain eye contact with at least three people: one on either side of the room and one in the middle. This gives the impression that you're looking at everyone. Smile; smiling will help to relax both you and your audience.

9 **During classes and lectures, ask permission to record part of what you hear on your smart phone or other recording device.** After class, listen to portions and improve your speaking skills by taking time to repeat what you have heard several times. This helps you with intonation patterns and the pronunciation of key words and expressions related to your teacher's ideas. This not only prepares you to discuss the ideas in class, but also serves as an effective study aid.

10 **When you are tested on speaking, it is often done as an interview in which you must also understand the questions you hear.** The most important thing is to ensure that you understand the question or speaking prompt. If you are not sure, politely ask for clarification. Take a moment to consider your answer and then focus on giving a complete answer. Don't try to say as little as possible to avoid making mistakes. If, part way through your answer, you realize you have misunderstood the question, ask for the chance to begin again. This is better than delivering an incomplete or wrong answer.

To really improve your English, take every opportunity to read, write, speak, and listen.

© ERPI • Reproduction prohibited

APPENDIX 4
Conversation Gambits

Gambits are commonly understood ways of starting, maintaining, and ending informal and formal conversations in polite ways. Practise the following on your own and with a partner.

GAMBITS	INFORMAL	FORMAL
OFFER GREETINGS	Hi. How are you?	Hello. How are you?
INTRODUCE A TOPIC	I'd like to talk to you about …	If you have a moment, I would like to discuss …
EXPLAIN A POINT	Let me explain. Here's the idea. What do you think about …?	Let me suggest … The basic idea is … The important part of the idea is …
CHECK FOR COMPREHENSION	Do you get what I'm saying? Do you follow what I've said so far?	May I ask if you understand my point? Is everything clear so far?
SHOW YOU ARE LISTENING	[frown/nod] Really? Right. Uh-huh. OK.	[frown/nod] Yes. Are you sure?
SHOW AGREEMENT	Yes. I agree. I can't argue with that.	Yes. I agree. That's true. You've made a good point.
INTERRUPT	I'm sorry, … Excuse me, … Pardon me, but … Can I ask a question? Can I add something here?	Sorry for interrupting, but … If I can just interrupt for a moment, … If I could stop you there for a second, …
ASK THE SPEAKER TO REPEAT	Can you say that again? Could you repeat that? What was that? Excuse me? Sorry, what?	I'm not sure I follow. Would you mind repeating that? Pardon me, what did you say?
REFUSE INTERRUPTIONS	Please, let me finish. Can I just finish my point?	Perhaps if you could let me finish. May I just finish my point?
CONTINUE AFTER AN INTERRUPTION	As I was saying, … Let's see, where was I?	To get back to what I was saying, …
DISAGREE POLITELY	That's not true/right, is it? I'd say/think something different …	I'm not sure I agree. I can't say that that's a convincing point/argument.
MAKE A QUALIFICATION	That's not totally what I meant.	Although I agree with …, I also believe …
EXPRESS AN OPINION	In my opinion, … What I think … As I see it, …	My personal opinion is that …
CLARIFY THE SPEAKER'S POINTS BY RESTATING	So, what you mean is … So, what you're trying to say is …	If I can restate, first you state … Then, I understand your point is …
CLARIFY YOUR POINTS BY RESTATING	What I'm trying to say is … What I mean is …	To put it another way, … Let me explain it another way …
SUMMARIZE	All in all, what I'm trying to say is … The main points are …	To summarize, … To bring all this together, …
END THE CONVERSATION	I have to go now, but it's been great talking with you. Thanks for the chance to talk.	I'm glad we had a chance to talk. Thank you for taking the time to speak with me.

© ERPI • Reproduction prohibited

PHOTO CREDITS

ALAMY
p. 87 (r) © Jeff Morgan 05.

ASKFORTASK.COM
p. 53.

DOSU STUDIO ARCHITECTURE
pp. 90 (b), 93, 94.

FOTOLIA
pp. viii, 2, 21 © Sergey Nivens; p. 3 © relif; p. 4 © Tyler Olson; p. 6 © WavebreakMediaMicro; p. 7 © GoneWithTheWind; p. 8 © Photobank; p. 11 (t) © Minerva Studio; p. 12 © maraduchetti; p. 13 © UBER IMAGES; p. 14 © Giorgio Pulcini; p. 15 © merla; p. 16 © artzenter; p. 19 (l) © Merijar; p. 19 (r) © Voyagerix; p. 20 © ecuadorquerido; pp. viii, 22, 39 © Damian; p. 23 © Henryk Sadura; p. 24 © kuco; p. 25 © chrisdorney; p. 26 © bst2012; p. 27 © vanila91; p. 29 (l) © Nataly-Nete; p. 29 (r) © ALDECAstudio; p. 31 © yellowj; p. 32 © flucas; p. 33 © alswart; p. 34 © nattaponsa; p. 35 © AfricaStudio; p. 38 © VadimGuzhva; pp. viii, 40, 57 © Irochka; p. 41 © juliabatsheva; p. 42 (r) © jozsitoeroe; p. 42 (l) © Marco Gabbin; p. 44 © Elenathewise; p. 45 © vege; p. 46 (t) © dimj; p. 46 (b) © winston; p. 47 © gentelmenit; p. 48 © Photographee.eu; p. 49 © JJAVA; p. 50 © eyalg_115; p. 54 (t) © Zarya Maxim; p. 54 (b) © bigshotd3; p. 55 © Monkey Business; p. 60 © netsuthep; p. 62 (l) © prudkov; p. 62 (r), 63 (l) © claudiociani; p. 63 (l,c) © scatto79; p. 63 (r,c) © Jacob Lund; p. 63 (r) © highwaystarz; p. 64 © dmitrimaruta; p. 65 © usamedeniz; p. 66 © adam121; p. 68 © Vadimsadovski; p. 70 © olly; p. 75 © cristovao31; pp. viii, 78, 97 © Oleksandr Kotenko; p. 80 © nastia1983; p. 81 (t) © kantver; p. 81 (b) © djvstock; p. 83 (t) © sss78; p. 83 (b) © lemontreeimages; p. 84 © Absoludesigner; p. 85 (t) © Tijana; p. 85 (b) © Helen Hotson; p. 86 © chika_milan; p. 87 (l) © korkorkorpai; p. 88 © FPWing; p. 90 (t,l) © mtaira; p. 90 (t,l,c) © Bill Perry; p. 90 (t,r,c) © Netfalls; p. 90 (t,r) © vachiraphan; p. 92 © Eduard Shelesnjak; p. 95 © freefly; pp. ix, 98, 117 © Sergey Nivens; p. 99 © bloomicon; p. 100 © Minerva Studio; p. 101 © Romolo Tavani; p. 103 © Sergii Figurnyi; p. 105 © BestPhotoStudio; p. 106 (t) © Sergey Nivens; p. 106 (b) © Christian Musat; p. 107 © olly; p. 108 © Joshua Resnick; p. 110 © toxicsalad; p. 111 (m) © aliaksei_7799; p. 111 (l) © Alexander Ozerov; p. 113 (t) © Rafael Ben-Ari; p. 113 (b) © Juulijs; p. 115 (l) © sergeyonas; p. 115 (r) © WavebreakmediaMicro; pp. ix, 118, 137 © funkyfrogstock; pp. 119, 120 (b) © KANDA EUATHAM; p. 120 (m) © Syda Productions; p. 121 © bubbers; p. 122 © sebra; p. 123 (t) © Olly; p. 123 (b) © Bitter; p. 124 © Tyler Olson; p. 125 © Melory; p. 126 © Monkey Business; p. 127 © vitaliy_melnik; p. 128 © Anatomy Insider; p. 130 © paultarasenko; p. 131 © bobakphoto; p. 132 © vasakna; p. 133 (l) © vectorchef; p. 133 (l,c) © photomelon; p. 133 (r,c) © sarawut_ch; p. 133 (r) © telmanbagirov; p. 134 © WavebreakmediaMicro; p. 135 © Saklakova; pp. ix, 138, 156 © Herschel Hoffmeyer; p. 139 © Giordano Aita; p. 140 © Leona Kali; p. 141 © Rawpixel.com; p. 142 (b) © Andrii IURLOV; p. 143 © niky002; p. 144 © nicolasprimola; p. 145 © Alliance; p. 146 © chagpg; p. 147 (t) © Catmando; p. 147 (b) © storm; p. 148 © Microgen; p. 149 © shock; p. 150 (t) © auntspray; p. 150 (b) © pressmaster; p. 151 © James Thew; p. 152 © SemA; p. 153 © alessandrozocc; p. 155 © Fujita.

JOHN KEALEY
p. 37.

NASA
pp. 71, 73.

WADE DAVIS
p. 112 © Nik West/Wade Davis.

WIKIMEDIA COMMONS
pp. 11 (b), 69, 142 (t), 154.

UNSPLASH.COM
pp. viii, 58, 77 © RhondaK.

© ERPI • Reproduction prohibited

VIDEO CREDITS

CHAPTER 1

p. 15 "How to Learn Anything, with Scott Young" © Ramit Sethi.

CHAPTER 2

p. 34 "Canadian Develops Futuristic Hoverboard" © Canadian Broadcasting Corporation.

CHAPTER 3

p. 53 "AskforTask CEO Interview" Lang and O'Leary Exchange © Canadian Broadcasting Corporation.

CHAPTER 4

p. 71 "Chris Hadfield, Hero Astronaut" George Stroumboulopoulos Tonight © Canadian Broadcasting Corporation.

CHAPTER 5

p. 91 "Buildings That Breathe: Doris Sung's Living Architecture" © VICE MEDIA LLC.

CHAPTER 6

p. 112 "The World View of Wade Davis" © Canadian Broadcasting Corporation

CHAPTER 7

p. 131 "How to Have a Good Day by Caroline Webb" © ProductivityGame.com (Nathan Lozeron).

CHAPTER 8

p. 151 "The Sixth Extinction: Interview with Elizabeth Kolbert" CBS This Morning © CBS News.

© **ERPI** • Reproduction prohibited

NOTES

© **ERPI** • Reproduction prohibited

© ERPI • Reproduction prohibited

© **ERPI** • Reproduction prohibited

© **ERPI** • Reproduction prohibited